On the Philosophy of Religion

Richard M. Gale
University of Pittsburgh, Professor Emeritus

THOMSON
— ✳ —™
WADSWORTH

Australia • Brazil • Canada • Mexico • Singapore • Spain
United Kingdom • United States

On the Philosophy of Religion
Richard M. Gale

Philosophy Editor: Steve Wainwright

Assistant Editors: Lee McCracken, Barbara Hillaker

Editorial Assistant: Patrick Stockstill

Technology Project Manager: Julie Aguilar

Marketing Manager: Worth Hawes

Marketing Assistant: Kathleen Tosiello

Marketing Communications Manager: Stacey Purviance

Creative Director: Rob Hugel

Executive Art Director: Maria Epes

Print Buyer: Nora Massuda

Permissions Editor: Roberta Broyer

Production Service/Compositor: Integra Software Services

Copy Editor: Sharon Green

Text and Cover Printer: West Group

Thomson Higher Education
10 Davis Drive
Belmont, CA 94002-3098
USA

For more information about our products, contact us at:
Thomson Learning Academic Resource Center
1-800-423-0563

For permission to use material from this text or product, submit a request online at http://www.thomsonrights.com. Any additional questions about permissions can be submitted by e-mail to thomsonrights@thomson.com.

Library of Congress Control Number: 2006932739

ISBN-13: 978-0-495-00914-6
ISBN-10: 0-495-00914-8

Dedication

For the grandchildren
Max, Sally, Michael, John, and Lauren

Contents

Preface

The aim of this book is to provoke give-and-take discussion, preferably heated, among undergraduate students taking a course in philosophy of religion. It discusses issues that usually appear in such a course and does so in a tennis match manner in which the polemical ball is followed as it gets batted back and forth between rivals, but unlike a real life tennis match there is no termination to the rallies. Through demonstration of the art of countering an argument with an argument, it is hoped that students will acquire the polemical skills to keep the discussion going. Most students, to be sure, will eventually exit the discussion but will do so with a clearer understanding of and better justification for what they believed when they initially entered into it.

The underlying question of this book is whether it is rational in some sense to believe that the God of traditional Western theism exists. This God is an absolutely perfect being, a being than which none greater is conceivable, and one eminently worthy of love, adoration, worship, and obedience. Two different ways of justifying a belief will be considered. One is based on arguments that are intended to support the truth of the proposition believed—that God exists—and will be called "evidential or epistemic justification." The success of these arguments is not dependent in any way upon the desires, values, and needs of people. A "nonevidentialist justification" does not support the truth of the proposition believed but instead argues that, overall, the consequences of having the belief are good. Thus, the success of such a justification, unlike an evidential justification, is crucially dependent upon the desires, values, and needs of people.

Before considering evidential and nonevidential justifications of theistic belief, it is necessary to clarify the concept of God, especially since it has given rise to puzzlement and perplexity, having been a rich breeding ground of paradox. Numerous arguments will be presented in Chapter 1 to show that the very concept of God is incoherent or contradictory. It will be seen how the attempts to escape them have led to a more sophisticated and viable conception of God's nature. Evidential justifications, consisting in arguments for God's existence, will be the topic of Chapter 2 Four of the most important arguments for God's existence will be critically evaluated, these being the ontological, cosmological, teleological, and religious experience arguments. It is important in evaluating these arguments that we avoid the divide-and-conquer strategy of considering each argument in isolation and showing that it alone does not succeed in adequately supporting theism. We must be willing to consider what results when all of the premises of these arguments are combined into one master argument. Just as each piece of evidence might not alone suffice to show that Jones committed the murder, their conjunction might do so. And, similarly, even though each argument alone fails to give adequate evidential support to theistic belief, their conjunction might do so. Chapter 3 will consider the problem of evil, which is the major evidential reason for doubting the existence of God. Again, it will be seen how refinements in our conception of God are needed if the theist is going to be able to meet this challenge. Chapter 4 will deal with nonevidential justifications for and against theistic belief, the most prominent of which is the pragmatic justification based upon the desirable consequences of believing that God exists.

It is not the intention of this book to promote any position on the belief versus nonbelief issue, to put a new song in anyone's heart, but instead to give students an experience of the delight and thrill of letting their minds roam free and follow arguments wherever they might lead. Philosophy is not a station that you get off at but a journey in which interesting landscape is illuminated as you proceed. If it greatly matters to you what station you get off at, I suggest that you ride the subway rather than do philosophy.

I thank my dear friend, Alexander Pruss, for having helped me immeasurably in getting clear about the issues in this book. In particular, I am indebted to him for supplying much of the more technical material in the section on the teleological argument. He was in name my student, but in reality I was his student. I am also indebted to Michael Hodges and Melvin Tuggle for their helpful suggestions on how to improve my book.

1

The Nature of God

Since the concern of this book is whether it is rational to believe that the God of traditional Western theism exists, it is essential that at the outset we get clear on what sort of a God this is, hence the topic of this chapter. It is especially important that we do so at this juncture in the history of philosophy, since the very meaningfulness of our talk about this God has been challenged by doctrines of meaning that have been developed in the twentieth century.

To begin with, it must be recognized that there are many different ways of conceiving of this God, running the gamut from the highly anthropomorphic in which God is conceived of in largely human terms to the ultra sophisticated. Each person's conception of God evolves as she[1] matures in a way that is similar in some respects to the historical evolution of the concept of God within the Western theistic community. The highly anthropomorphic God of the Bible as a glorified avenger who periodically intercedes in history to wreak havoc on us for our sinful ways has become increasingly more sophisticated, with fewer and fewer terms that apply to human beings being literally applied to God. This sophisticating of our concept of God, as is the case of our sophisticating our concept of Santa Claus in which Santa Claus is downgraded to the level of the spirit of goodwill and generosity at Christmas, is needed so as to avoid straightforward falsification by experience of God's existence. (No, you didn't see

---

1 Feminine pronouns are used in Chapters 1 and 3 and male ones in
  Chapter 2 and 4 so as to avoid undue wordiness.

Mommy kissing Santa Claus, just your father dressed up as Santa Claus, although Mommy might not have known that!)

The great medieval theists went whole hog in their deanthropomorphizing of the personal God of the Scriptures through their metaphysicalizing of God in accordance with the Greek conception of what constitutes true being. This God is not only a purely spiritual, supernatural being but an absolutely simple, timeless, immutable, and self-subsistent being as well. The worry is that this fancy God has been drained of all personal characteristics and thus is not able, as is the God of the Scriptures, to be personally involved with his creatures, periodically, warning, consoling, and directing them, and occasionally revealing himself directly to them in mystical experiences. But this worry about the religious availability of the God of these medieval theists to the working theist should not worry us too much once it is realized that their conception of God is a theoretical reconstruction of the Biblical God and is as remote from it as the atomic theory of matter is from the medium-sized dry goods of our gross sense experience. The upshot is that we should not shy away from departing from their concept if there are good reasons for doing so. Progress is made in all areas of human endeavor. Theology and philosophy should not be exceptions.

According to this medieval concept, God is an absolutely perfect being and thus must possess every unlimited perfection, among which are being all-powerful (omnipotent), all-knowing (omniscient), all-good (omnibenevolent), sovereign over all, eternal, and immutable. Each of these perfections historically has been the basis of an "atheological argument," which is an argument that attempts to deduce an explicit contradiction from a set of initial premises accepted by the theist, one of which involves attributing the perfection in question to God. An explicit contradiction is of the form p and not-p, in which p is some proposition, such as that human beings are bipeds and that it is not the case that human beings are bipeds. In a contradiction it must be the case that one of the propositions is true and the other is false. In the course of this deduction, additional premises can be employed provided they are necessarily true. The propositions that an object is on Earth at one time and that this object is on the Moon a second later are not logically incompatible propositions; for the negation of the latter can be deduced from the former only if the *contingently* true additional premises are added, namely, that an object cannot travel faster than 186,000 miles per second and that the Moon is 239,000 miles from Earth, in which a contingent proposition is both possibly true and possibly false. That this object is on the Earth at a certain time and that it is on the Moon at that very same time are incompatible propositions in virtue of the impossibility of an object simultaneously occupying two different places. These atheological arguments hang the theist by her own rope. Historically, they have had the constructive purpose of forcing the theist to go back to the drawing board and redesign her conception of God so as to escape the deduced contradiction. To reestablish consistency in her web of belief, the theist must give up or alter one or more of the propositions in the initial set. This will become clear as we consider different atheological arguments.

OMNIPOTENCE

The simplest of all atheological arguments is directed against God's omnipotence. The initial set of propositions is comprised of these two propositions.

1. God is essentially omnipotent.
O. It is necessary that, for any proposition p, if God wills that p, then p.

Because premise 1 is true by definition, God essentially has the property of being omnipotent, which means that he could not exist without having this property. Premise O, in turn, gives a definition or analysis of what it is for God to be omnipotent that places no limitations or restrictions on God's omnipotence. This analysis, supposedly, brings out what our concept of God's omnipotence is and thus is some kind of a necessary conceptual or logical truth. This notion of logical or conceptual necessity defies definition; however, clear-cut examples of a logically or conceptually necessary proposition can be given, such as that two and two are four, that a physical object is extended (to which Hector Castenada gave the counterexample of I went to kiss Mary but her lips were not extended). Under no conceivable or imaginable circumstances could a necessarily true proposition be false. A conceptually or logically impossible proposition is one that under no conceivable or imaginable circumstances could be true.

Since O places no restriction on God's omnipotence, it must be possible for God to create a stone so heavy that God cannot lift it. But this entails that God might not be omnipotent and therefore is not essentially omnipotent; for in the case in which he exercises this potentiality, there is a task that he cannot do, which violates his being *essentially* omnipotent. And, if he cannot create this stone, he again fails to be omnipotent since there is a task that he cannot do. Thus, in each case, he fails to be essentially omnipotent, which contradicts the first proposition in the initial set that requires God to be essentially omnipotent. God both is and is not essentially omnipotent.

There is a radical way of dealing with this atheological argument that saves God's unrestricted omnipotence—allow God to do or bring about contradictory things. Thus, he can create the stone, but he also can lift it. Because God is the determiner of everything, including the laws of logic, he cannot be limited by them. There is a good reason why almost no theist of note has gone this route (and even Descartes is not a clear example, since he can be read as saying only that God cannot be limited by what we humans take to be logically possible since our intuitions about such matters could be mistaken), namely, we are so psychologically constituted that we cannot get ourselves to believe what we take to be contradictory. A Hollywood producer would reject a script that allows God to do or bring about the contradictory by saying "It's great, baby, but who'd believe it." And he would be right. Furthermore, as everyone who has taken Introduction to Logic knows, a contradiction entails that every proposition is true. And, again, that's more than people can get themselves to believe.

Obviously, the theist must place some restriction on God's omnipotence. She should not shy away from doing so once she realizes that the theologian's concept of God's omnipotence in terms of O is a theoretical reconstruction of the Biblical claim that God is all-mighty because his will cannot fail to be efficacious. The most obvious move is to restrict O to logically possible propositions, thus giving us

O_1. Necessarily, for any logically possible proposition, p, if God wills that p, then p.

That there is a stone so heavy that God, an essentially omnipotent being, cannot lift it is not logically possible, and thus God is excused from having to be able to bring it about, thereby saving his omnipotence.

There are, however, logically possible propositions, such as that God exists and that there exists an uncreated stone, which it would be logically contradictory for God to bring about. If God were to bring it about that there exists an uncreated stone, there would exist a stone that is both created and uncreated, surely a contradiction. Thus, yet another restriction on God's omnipotence is required, namely a restriction to what it is logically consistent for God to bring about.

O_2. Necessarily, for any proposition, p, such that it is logically possible that God bring it about that p, God can bring it about that p.

The reason for the use of the "bring about" rather than "do" terminology is that God, in virtue of being an immaterial being, does not perform actions like riding a bicycle or making love to the girl next door. Rather he brings it about by his will that a bicycle is ridden or that the girl next door is made love to. This way of restricting God's omnipotence will be seen in Chapter 2 to figure prominently in various attempts to show how God could be justified in creating free persons who sometimes do what is morally wrong; for, supposedly, it would be logically inconsistent for God to both create free persons and determine what they freely do.

Even O_2 is not problem free. Some would charge it with unduly restricting God's freedom, since it precludes God's acting immorally, both of which are logically impossible for him to do given that he is essentially omnibenevolent. God's freedom, like his omnipotence, must be restricted to what it is consistent for God, an absolutely perfect being, to do. This has results that some see as paradoxical. For God, in virtue of being an absolutely perfect being, will have a lesser degree of omnipotence and freedom than that possessed by a possible nonperfect being. It can perform all of God's parlor tricks, such as creating a universe *ex nihilo*, but in addition, since not omnibenevolent, can do what is immoral. (It should be pointed out that Saint Thomas Aquinas would deny that, on the basis of the Divine simplicity that holds all of God's properties to be one and the same, that a being could possess one but not all of God's perfections.) God pays a price for his perfection. Being perfect, he cannot be physical, which precludes him from riding a bicycle or making love to the girl next door. Maybe this goes to show that no one is perfect. Is this a case of anthropomorphism having gone amuck?

Another problem with O_2's relativizing God's omnipotence to what it is consistent for God to do is that it makes it too easy for other beings to qualify as omnipotent when their omnipotence is relativized to what it is consistent for them to do. Let a "pirod," by definition, be a being that can bring it about only that a pencil exists. Intuitively, a pirod has very little creative power, but a pirod counts as omnipotent in the subject–relativized sense: It can bring about anything that it is logically consistent for it, a pirod, to bring about. The response to this might be that there is a world of difference between restricting omnipotence to what it is consistent for a perfect being to do and what it is consistent for a pirod to do.

IMMUTABILITY

Another Divine attribute according to the great medieval theists, which also has bred paradox, is that of strict immutability. This requirement for being a perfect being was based on considerations derived from Plato and Aristotle. Plato reasoned that any change in a being that already is perfect would be a deterioration, thereby over-looking the possibility that the result of a change might be neutral: If I change my clothes, I need not thereby becomes better or worse. Aristotle held that a perfect being had already arrived and therefore had no unrealized possibilities, which precludes its changing. Herein is an expression of the Greeks's disdain for time and change, which they relegated to the less real world of becoming. This prejudice in favor of immutability has been challenged in modern times by numerous process philosophers, including James, Bergson, and Dewey, culminating in the process theology of Alfred North White-head. God's strict immutability, however, allowed him to change with respect to his nonintrinsic properties, the ones that he has in virtue of his relation to other things, for example, to change from being thought about by Jones at one time but not at another. This makes no real change in God, though it does in Jones.

The Manicheans developed an atheological argument, the "creation-immutability" argument, to show that there is a contra-diction between the propositions that God is essentially immutable and that, as the Bible holds, he created the universe at some past time. These propositions form the initial set of propositions accepted by the theist. The argument proceeds by pointing out that, prior to the time at which the universe came into being, God was not exercising his creative powers but subsequently he was, thus occasioning an intrinsic change in God. And this contradicts the theist's claim that God is immutable. A succinct enthymemic way to formulate this argument is "What was God doing before he created the universe?" Saint

Augustine responded that "He was preparing the fires of hell for those who would ask this question."

The good Saint shows that he is not without levity, but he realized that this knee-slapper response did not neutralize the creation-immutability argument. Contending that time requires change, he denied that there was any time before God created the universe. The perspicuous, nonparadoxical way of putting this is that there is no time that is earlier than the time at which the universe came into being, thereby avoiding reference to times at which there was no time. In creating a universe of changing things, he thereby created time as well. The creation-immutability argument, however, can be reformulated in terms of an intra-universe change consisting in something happening or existing at one time but not at another, such as a stone existing at one time but not at another. Since God is continually creating the universe by sustaining it in existence, he wills something at one time, that the stone exists, that he does not will at another, thereby violating his essential immutability.

Fortunately, Augustine's real rebuttal of the argument is not based on the fact that there is no time before the universe came into existence. It is that God is a timeless being in the sense of not being subject to any temporal determinations or distinctions: He does not endure in or occupy time nor stand in any temporal relation to anything in time. His creative acts are not earlier or later than or temporally simultaneous with any worldly event or time. The fatal flaw in the creation-immutability argument is the unstated assumption that God's creative act is temporally simultaneous with its temporal effect, thereby placing God's creative acts in time, the very same time that its effects occupy. God exists in an eternal now that has no contrast with a past and future, and all of his creative acts occur within it. The effects of these timeless acts occur in time. Because there is no succession within God's creative acts of will, although there is within some of the worldly effects of these acts, God's immutability is not compromised by his being the creator of a temporal universe, even one that has a beginning in time.

Many theists would not accept this way out of the creation-immutability argument since they reject the viability of the concept of God's timeless eternality and causation, opting instead for the Biblical conception of God's eternality as involving omnitemporality— endurance throughout a beginningless and endless time without the possibility of beginning or ceasing to exist. It is not required that this God be absolutely immutable. Not only does he grow older (at any time he is infinitely old!) but he is allowed to change in his nonessential properties, even ones that are nonrelational. The dispute between the friends and foes of Divine timelessness is a long-lasting one that represents a deep parting of the ways since it gets down to what kind of God we want, some wanting a somewhat anthropomorphic deity with which they can personally interact and others a mystical God that is accessible only through mystical experiences. Put in a nutshell, the foes of Divine timelessness want a God who is religiously available to agents, whereas the friends of Divine timelessness want a God with whom they can mystically commune. The latter will have the features of the content of a unitive mystical experience—timelessness, immutability, ineffability and simplicity—while the former will be of a kind with which worldly agents can interact. We want both of these gods, and the challenge to the theologian is to find some way to unify them, as, for example, by some mystical doctrine like that of the Trinity. It will be seen that it is doubtful that the God of agency is amenable to the same analysis as is appropriate for the mystical God, and thus doubtful that the former can have the latter's timeless eternality. It will be instructive in this connection to consider the polemical exchanges between them.

We have already seen the arguments of Plato and Aristotle for why the highest being must be timeless and immutable that were employed by the friends of Divine timelessness. Another supporting argument, supplied by Saint Anselm, holds that a greatest conceivable being must be timeless for if it were *in* time it would have at least the possibility of beginning or ending and thereby fail to qualify as a greatest conceivable being. A foe of timelessness will reject this argument because it is based on a hasty generalization from ordinary temporal beings.

The proponents of Divine omnitemporal eternality have mounted a three-prong attack on the concept of a timelessly eternal God. The first prong charges this concept with being meaningless. To begin with, the doctrine of God's timeless causation of events in time has been charged with being conceptually vacuous. Unlike the cases of causation that we are familiar with in our ordinary experience, there is no temporal relation of precedence or simultaneity between the cause and its effect, nor is there any law-like or nomic backing when God timelessly brings about a worldly effect: His causing something to exist or happen is not an instance of some universal causal law of science. But that there are these differences between ordinary and Divine causation should not surprise us, given that you could say of God, in the lingo of the street, "Man, he's something else." And you'd be right since he is completely other, completely out of it, wholly other. We must be on guard against the fallacy of "the legislativeness of ordinary language," in which the ordinary use of a word is legislative for all uses of it; any use of a word that departs from its seminal ordinary use being incorrect, a misuse of language. For the fact that we have never had the occasion to say something (that two gorillas are waltzing together) does not show that it would be conceptually wrong, violating a "rule" of language, to say it. Thus, it is dubious to infer from the fact that all the causal relations we know of involve a temporal relation between cause and effect that it is conceptually impossible for God to timelessly bring about effects in time. And the fact that the individuals to whom we ordinarily ascribe personal traits have physical bodies should not preclude our extending these traits to an immaterial individual, such as God. This needed jump from what we actually say to what it is conceptually correct to say is the bane of ordinary language philosophy or conceptual analysis.

There is, however, a special problem of God's timeless creation that is not based on the legislativeness of ordinary language. It concerns how it is possible for God to create time, as he is claimed to do by Augustine. One cannot intentionally create or bring about what she does not understand. But God, in virtue of being timeless, cannot understand what time is and therefore cannot create it or any successive events in time. To understand what time is requires understanding the temporal relation of succession or earlier than. Only someone who has had an experience of succession can understand it, just as only someone who has experienced yellow can understand what it is. God can know the logical properties of earlier than, that it is a relation that is irreflexive (nothing is earlier than itself), transitive (if x is earlier than y and y is earlier than z, then x is earlier than z), and asymmetric (if x is earlier than y, then y is not earlier than x); but this does not distinguish it from certain nontemporal relations, such as larger than. Thus, when God says "Let there be time," he has no idea of what he is talking about. (If he were to have said, "Let there be time, whatever the hell that is," what would have resulted?)

A further problem with timeless causation is that it seems to violate our gut intuition that there must be as much reality in the cause as in its effect. Whatever exists in the effect must exist, at least potentially, in the cause. This requirement is driven by the idea that the cause must be explanatorily adequate for its effect. What is time-less does not seem explanatorily adequate for its temporal effect in the same way that a temporal cause is not explanatorily adequate for a timeless effect, for example, a human action causing God to timelessly be aware of it. Although something could come out of nothing, not have any cause, it could not be caused to do so by nothing. It is interesting to note that the very same medieval philosophers who bought in on the principle that there must be as much reality in the cause as in its effect also accepted the doctrine of Divine timeless causation of temporal effects. It was for this reason that they denied that an event in time could causally affect God, but they should have seen that the same reasoning precludes a timeless act from having a temporal effect.

The concept of God's timeless existence also is not without difficulties. God resembles the abstract entities, such as properties, ideas, forms, and propositions, that populate Plato's heaven in that, like these abstracta, he is not locatable in space and time and thus is not subject to the gnawing tooth of time, remaining just as young, sweet, and innocent as he always was: "Neither time can wither nor custom stale," as the graduation oration has it. But he differs from them in that he is a person and thus must have a life, but it is a funny one because it occurs in a single eternal now without any succession. He is said by Boethius and Augustine to enjoy an illimitable life that consists in a timeless duration in which all of his years are had all at once. All his actions occur within an eternal present—a present that has no contrasting past or future—and he is copresent with every worldly time.

It is objected that a "timeless duration" is a contradiction in terms. Furthermore, the years that comprise one's life are, by definition, successive; and the concept of an eternal now is mean-ingless since it lacks the needed contrast with the past and future. By withdrawing this significant contrast, language is made to idle, just as it would if we retained the use of the first person but withdrew from the language the needed contrast with the second and third person. And for good measure, a timeless being cannot be copresent or simultaneous with a worldly time, since, by definition, "simultaneity" and "copresence" mean existence or occurrence at the same time.

What response could be made to these charges of conceptual incoherence by the friends of Divine timelessness? Again, the legislativeness of ordinary language is the main bone of contention. Ordinary language is used to describe God's timeless eternality, but it is used in an extraordinary way. Students who have some background in the literature of mysticism will be struck by the similarity between the descriptions that mystics give of their monistic mystical experiences in which complete union is achieved with God or the Eternal One and the description of God's timeless eternality. In both cases, the language used abounds in apparent contradictions. But mystics claim that one who has had a mystical experience or has a heightened sense of mystical awareness can understand what is said. I remember saying to Daisetzu Suzuki, the man who was instrumental in popularizing Zen in the West, that the Zen doctrine of the eternal now— that there is only the present—is meaningless because it withdraws from the language the needed significant contrast with past and future, to which he replied that from the standpoint of ordinary language it is meaningless but nevertheless it is a fact!

The second prong of the attack on the doctrine of God's timeless eternality attempts to show that a person conceptually cannot be timeless. All parties to the dispute agree that God must be a person; and, even though they disagree about the niceties of the analysis of the concept of personhood, which is not surprising given that the concept is largely a forensic one that has to do with the features of persons that make them morally and legally responsible, they agree that at a minimum a person have reason, which involves being conscious, having memories, knowledge and beliefs, as well as the capacity to act intentionally. In other words, a person must be a rational agent. The friends and foes of Divine timelessness have opposed intuitions about whether it is conceptually possible for a timeless being to have these rationality and agency properties. The foes appeal to "ordinary language" to support their modal intuitions, for the beings of which we ordinarily predicate these properties are temporal. For example, the foes would reject on conceptual grounds the imputation of purposeful action to a timeless God, since ordinary, familiar cases of purposeful action have the fulfillment of the purpose come later than the action; but for a timeless God there is no temporal relation between his timeless act and its worldly fulfillment. Again, we run up against rival intuitions about the legislativeness of ordinary language.

To begin with, consciousness, at least of the more developed sort that is required of a person, is a process, something that goes on, and therefore is temporal. The friends of Divine timelessness attempt to show that their timeless God can have specific forms of consciousness, such as memory and belief and purpose, which would entail being conscious. Having memory certainly is essential for any more developed sort of consciousness. Ordinarily, we say that someone remembers only if what is remembered is earlier than the remembering, and therefore a timeless God cannot have such ordinary memories and thus cannot be conscious. To meet this difficulty, Paul Helm concocted a timeless analogue to ordinary temporal memory which God can have. Whereas ordinary remembering is knowing that p and having not forgotten that p, a timeless being remembers p when he knows p and it is impossible for him to forget.

This contrived timeless analogue to ordinary memory is suspect. The only part of Helm's definition that specifically concerns memory is the clause that "it is impossible for God to forget p." But it is true also of the number seven, that it is impossible for it to forget p. Are we then to say that there is a number analogue to memory? Seven "remembers" being odd just in case seven is odd, and it is impossible for it to forget being odd.

There are psychological states, such as believing, knowing, intending, and loving, that go on in a homogeneous manner, being complete at every time at which a person is in such a state. Because they do not involve that their subjects undergo any change or process, it has been contended by the friends of Divine timelessness that their God could have them and thereby have a sufficiently rich psychology so as to qualify as a person. The problem with this way of saving their God's personhood is that these psychological states require that their subject have dispositions to act in various ways, for example, for the person in love to act so as to protect the beloved, for the believer to act on her belief. But a timeless God cannot have any dispositions, since then it would have the possibility of changing, which violates its essential immutability. Also, these states endure in time and can begin and end, which are other reasons why this God couldn't be in them.

But even if the timeless God is a person, there remains the question of whether he is the right sort of person for the needs of the working theist who wants an eminently worshipable being with whom she can have personal interactions. And this brings us to the third prong of the attack of the omnitemporalists on the timelessly eternal deity. It attempts to show that this God lacks omniscience in a way that disqualifies it from playing this role.

OMNISCIENCE

This attack begins with the omniscience-timelessness atheological argument, whose initial set is comprised of these three propositions:

1. God is timelessly eternal.
2. God is omniscient, that is, he knows every true proposition and believes only true ones.
3. There are true tensed propositions that report events as being past (present, future).

But, in virtue of the fact that God is timeless it follow that

4. God does not know these true tensed propositions. From 1 and 3

From which it follows that

5. God is not omniscient. From 4

Therefore,

6. God is omniscient and God is not omniscient. From 2 and 5

Some explanations and justifications for steps 3 and 4 are needed. Western theism, unlike Buddhism, accepts the reality of time, and among the patent temporal facts that are vouchsafed by our experience is that some event is occurring now, at present, while other events have occurred, are past, and others are about to occur, are future. But why is a timeless God barred from knowing such tensed facts? In order to know a proposition one must be able to express it. Assume that the tensed proposition that it is raining now is true. Only a being who exists at this very present moment of time can express this proposition, which bars God from knowing this proposition. But what is meant by *express*? A timeless being can timelessly bring it about that a tensed sentence is inscribed or uttered at a certain time. Think of a parallel case involving a spatial indexical sentence containing "here." A being who is not here, or maybe not even in space at all, could cause it to be the case that an inscribing or uttering of the sentence "The treasure is here" occurs at a certain place. Think of a ventriloquist. Why couldn't there be a temporal ventriloquist? It might be countered that, although he causes an inscription or uttering of a tensed sentence at a certain time, he does not *express* the tensed proposition because he cannot understand it, since he doesn't exist at the time in question. But this is the first explanation and thus brings us full circle. Maybe the second answer can be bolstered by analogy with the personal indexical proposition that "I am Richard Gale." Even if some ventriloquist were to cause it to be the case that the sounds made by an uttering of the sentence "I am Richard Gale" were to emanate from my mouth, she would fail to express the very same proposition that would be expressed by my uttering the sentence.

There are responses to the omniscience-timelessness argument. The first argues that a timeless God can know a tensed proposition by knowing some tenseless proposition that is either identical with or entails it. Assume that it is now t_4. God can know the tenseless proposition that it rains (tenselessly) at t_4. This proposition is identical with the tensed proposition that it is raining now, and thus in knowing the former he also knows the latter. The response to this way out of the omniscience-timelessneess argument is that these propositions are not identical, since one could know or believe one of them but not the other. For example, you could know that it is raining now without knowing that it rains (tenselessly) at t_4, and vice versa. We often don't know what the date is.

There are two other responses that also seem to require too little of God's omniscience. That it rains (tenselessly) at t_4 reports one and the same event as does that it is raining now; for, given that now = t_4, it's raining now is one and the same event as its raining at t_4. Therefore, God knows of "its raining now" only under that description but not under the description "its raining at t_4." But an omniscient being must not just know of the occurrence of every event but know of it under every description that is true of it, that is, he must know every proposition that truly reports the occurrence of the event.

Here is yet another strategy for escaping the argument. It will be recalled that it was found reasonable to restrict God's omnipotence to what it is logically consistent for him to bring about. If a similar restriction is placed upon God's omniscience, namely, 2′, God knows every true proposition that it is logically consistent for him to know. God is excused from having to know tensed propositions, since it is logically impossible for him to know them. This move creates an especially virulent version of the paradox of perfection, since it makes it too easy to be omniscient. Let our pirod now be defined as a being who knows only that grass is green. You wouldn't want to call him omniscient just because he knows every true proposition that it is logically consistent for him to know. Again, the response will be that there is a world of difference between restricting omniscience to what it is logically consistent for God, a greatest conceivable being, to know and to what it is consistent for a radically limited being like a pirod to know.

It will turn out that a timeless God's inability to know tensed propositions will seriously undermine his religious availability to working theists who pray to and commune with God through their apparent experiences of him. But before delving into this, the response of the friends of timeless eternality to the three-prong attack of the omnitemporalists will be considered.

One response is the plague-on-all-your-houses one, being like the baritone, who after being thoroughly booed by the notoriously tough Parma audience for his opera-opening aria, responded ,"If you think I stink, wait till you hear the tenor."

Whereas the timeless God fell prey to the omniscience-timelessness atheological argument, the omnitemporal God is a suitable target for the omniscience–immutability atheological argument. Its initial set is comprised of these four propositions:

1. God is omnitemporally eternal.

2. God is immutable.

3. God is omniscient, that is, he knows every true proposition and believes only true ones.

4. There are true-tensed propositions that report events as being past (present, future).

But,

5. In order to know every true-tensed proposition, God must change the way in which he expresses these propositions from one time to another. Premise

And, therefore,

6. God is not immutable. From 5

7. God is immutable and God is not immutable. From 2 and 6

To understand why 5 is true, imagine again that it rains at a time, t_4, but not before or after t_4. Being omniscient, God will believe prior to t_4 a proposition that is expressible by the English sentence "It will rain," or its synonym in his Deitese language, and at t_4 a proposition expressible by "It is now raining," and after t_4 a proposition expressible by "It was raining." Thus God must continually change the manner in which he expresses true-tensed propositions so as to literally remain up to date. God does not change his mind in the sense of believing a proposition that he formerly disbelieved, which would violate his omniscience since one of the two beliefs will be false, but only the manner in which he expresses his beliefs.

This plague-on-all-your-houses response unwittingly sets the stage for this dilemma argument for God's nonexistence.

1. God is essentially omniscient. Tenet of theism
2. God is essentially immutable. Tenet of theism
3. Either God is timelessly eternal or God is omnitemporally eternal. Premise
4. If God is timelessly eternal, he fails to know tensed propositions and thereby is not omniscient. Supported by the omniscience-timelessness atheological argument
5. If God is omnitemporally eternal, he changes in the way he expresses his beliefs and thereby fails and is not immutable. Supported by the omniscience-immutability atheological argument
6. Either God is not omniscient or God is not immutable. From 3, 4, and 5
7. God does not exist. From 1, 2, and 6

The reason why 7 follows from 1, 2, and 6 is that being omniscient and being immutable are each an essential property of God, a property in the absence of which he does not exist. It looks like that theist must be willing to water down either God's omniscience or his immutability. Reasons for thinking that the latter is the less painful way to go will be advanced shortly.

One consideration that has been advanced in favor of the timelessly eternal God is that it enables us to escape the omniscience-freedom atheological argument that the omnitemporally eternal God *cannot*. A crude version of it was given by Boethius that committed a blatant mistake in its way of spelling out God's omniscience. The argument begins with this initial set of propositions accepted by the theist.

1. God is omnitemporally eternal.
2. God is essentially omniscient.
3. There are creatures who sometimes perform free actions.

The argument then proceeds as follows:

4. For any action that a creature performs God believes before this action occurs that it will occur. From 1, 2, and 3

5. Let *A* be any free action of a creature. Assumption

6. God believes before *A* occurs that *A* will occur. From 4 and 5

7. If God believes a proposition, then it is necessary that it is true. From 2

8. It is necessary that it is true that *A* will occur. From 6 and 7 by modus ponens (If *p* then *q*, *p*, therefore *q*)

9. *A* is not a free action. From 8

10. It is not the case that there are creatures who sometimes perform free actions. From 5 and 9

11. There are creatures who sometimes perform free actions, and it is not the case that there are creatures who sometimes perform free actions. From 3 and 10

The reason why 10 follows from 5 and 9 is that, since action *A* is an arbitrarily selected free action, whatever holds true for it holds true for every free action.

The advantage of making God timeless is that step 4 will no longer be derivable and thus the free actions of creatures will not be endangered by God having a prior, freedom-canceling belief that they will occur. This advantage of the timeless God over the omnitemporal one is illusory, since the argument is easily reformulated so as to apply to the timeless God. All that needs to be done is to replace 1, 5, and 7, respectively, by

1′. God is timelessly eternal.

4′. For every action that a creature performs (including free ones), God timelessly believes that this action occurs.

6′. God timelessly believes that *A* will occur.

And because of 7, it again follows that it is necessary that these actions occur. Thus, it makes no difference whether God's belief occurs temporally prior to the action in question or in his timeless present.

Even if Boethius's argument were to favor the timeless over the omnitemporal deity, it would not help the cause of the friends of God's timeless eternality since it is seriously flawed. In step 3—If God believes a proposition, then it is necessary that it be true—the "it is necessay" operator is placed incorrectly before the consequent proposition of the conditional proposition, the one that follows the "then," when it should be applied to the entire conditional, resulting in

7'. It is necessary that (if God believes a proposition, then it be true).

The parentheses indicate that the necessity operator has the entire if-then proposition within its scope. What is necessary is the connection between the antecedent and consequent. Whereas the conjunction of 7 with

8. Before A occurs, God believes that A will occur.

entailed

9. It is necessary that it is true that A will occur.

The conjunction of 7' with 8 does not entail 9. The argument form, "It is necessary that (if p, then q) and p, therefore it is necessary that q," is invalid. If it were valid, it could be deduced that every contingently true proposition is necessarily true. For every contingent proposition, p, it is necessary that (if p, then p). Given that p is true, it would then follow that it is necessary that p. From the conjunction of 7' and 8 it can be deduced only that

9'. It is true that A will occur.

But there is nothing freedom-canceling about this.

There is an improved version of Boethius' argument, credit due to Nelson Pike, that avoids Boethius's blunder and applies only to the omnitemporal deity, thus scoring a point in favor of the timeless deity. This argument assumes that God is omnitemporal and that propositions predicting the free actions of creatures are true or false in advance of the predicted action. God, being omniscient, foreknows and thereby believes in advance of a creaturely free action—that this creature will perform this action. It is then pointed out, if I may simplify his argument, that because this creature acts freely it has the power to refrain from doing that which God believes she will do. If the creature *were* to exercise this power and refrain from doing the predicted action, though it doesn't, the essentially omniscient God being would believe other than he actually does. But this means that this creature has the power to bring it about that God would believe other than he in fact does. But this sort of backward causation is a conceptual impossibility, and thus she does not have this power and thereby is not free with respect to the action in question.

One way to escape the clutches of this argument is to make God timelessly eternal, thereby precluding his having any beliefs about creaturely actions that are earlier than these actions. Another way is to show that there is a special type of counterexample to the claim that causation cannot go backward and that God's predictive belief is of that type. A present action can bring about a past fact when it is a "temporally impure fact" in that it places demands on what happens or fails to happen at times other than that at which the action occurs, examples of which are that yesterday Jones danced the first day of a ten-day dance, that Jones drank the fatal glass of beer one hour ago. I can now act so as to bring it about that these things did not occur by now preventing Jones from continuing his dance and pumping out his stomach. Because God is essentially omniscient, that he has a predictive belief at a certain time, entails that the fact that is predicted come to pass at a later time, thus qualifying it as a temporally impure fact. That a nonomniscient person *believes* that some event will occur is not a temporally impure fact, since it does not entail that this event *will* occur.

The friends of timeless eternality have another way of dealing with the problem posed by their God's inability to know tensed propositions that is worth critically examining in detail, especially since it gets to the heart of their dispute with the omnitemporalists regarding the religious availability of their respective gods. It is a parody in which atheological arguments exactly like the omniscience-timelessness argument are constructed for spatial and personal propositions that are analogues to tensed propositions. These propositions use, in place of temporal indexical terms like "now" and "the present," the spatial indexical term "here" and the personal indexical term "I," respectively. Just as "now" denotes the time at which it is uttered, "here" denotes the place at which it is uttered and "I" the person who utters it. Supposedly, these parody arguments stink, thereby showing that the omniscience-timelessness arguments should be discounted. This is the general form of these parody arguments:

(i) These parallel arguments have absurd consequences by the standards of traditional theism, and thus should be rejected by the theist.

(ii) The argument against a timeless God's omniscience based on tensed propositions also should be rejected by the theist. From (i) and (ii) by the principles of analogical reasoning

Premise (i), at first glance, looks right; for, just as tensed propositions are expressed through the use of sentences that are not freely
repeatable across times, spatial and personal indexical propositions are
expressible by sentences that are not freely repeatable, respectively,
across places and persons. Furthermore, just as one must exist now in
order to know the tensed proposition that it is raining *now*, one must
exist *here* and be identical with me to know, respectively, the propositions that the treasure is *here* and that *I am* Richard Gale. But it
would be absurd, according to traditional theism, to say that God is
numerically identical with his creatures or that he occupies some
place. Thus, theists must excuse God from having to know spatial
and personal indexical propositions; and, given the strong analogy
between these propositions and tensed propositions, they should do
likewise for tensed propositions. The proponents of the timeless God
challenge those who think it is important for God to know tensed
propositions, but not these personal and spatial indexical propositions,
to produce relevant disanalogies between them. This is a challenge
that is well worth accepting.

It must be granted at the outset that it is impossible for God to
know every true indexical proposition of any one of the three types—
temporal, spatial, and personal. But this leaves open whether this God
must know at least some true indexical propositions, and, if so, of
which of the three types must he have this knowledge. And if he must
have this knowledge for any given type, he must have the indexical
perspective that is required for having this knowledge. It would be a
howler to infer from the fact that God cannot know every true
indexical proposition of a certain type that he cannot know any one
of them, or even, that it is not required that he know some of them.
An argument will be given for why God must know some temporal
and personal indexical propositions but need not and cannot have
knowledge of any spatial one. And thus there is a very significant
disanalogy between temporal and personal indexicals, on the one
hand, and spatial indexicals, on the other.

It is obvious that God, being a person, must be capable of making
a first person indexical reference to himself, as for example by tokening "I am God" or whatever sentence in Deitese has the same meaning. And thus God will know at least some true personal indexical
propositions. If he is a purely spiritual being, then he is barred from
having any spatial indexical perspective and therefore from knowing
any spatial indexical proposition, since only a being in space can
express such a proposition. This does not hold if God becomes

incarnate as in the doctrine of the Trinity, but this is an issue that won't be pursued since it requires that sense be made of the doctrine of the Trinity, which is too tall an order for this book.

There is another reason why it is crucial to the role played by the personal God of the Bible, the one that interacts with men, that he have a personal indexical perspective. This is a requirement for his being able to have relations of intimacy with them. He must be able to *you* our *I*'s and we, in turn, *you* his *I*. While God cannot know the very proposition I express when I say "I am Richard Gale," he can know a different indexed counterpart proposition that entails the former, namely "He is Richard Gale," said as he ostends me. This mutually *I-you*-ing, or, as some would say, *I-thou*-ing, is necessary for personal dialogue.

Must God also have a unique spatial perspective for him to have intimate dialogue with men? No, for we can imagine having an intimate relation with a purely spiritual being. This is just what a séance is attempting to achieve. *Here* and *I*, therefore, are disanalogous with respect to our concept of intimacy, thereby undermining the analogical premise, (i), in the general form of the parody argument. An individual's not being in space does preclude some forms of intimate interaction.

Here also is disanalogous with *now* with respect to intimacy, which further undermines (i). For you can have an intimate dialogue or interaction with someone only if you assume that your temporal perspectives coincide—that she is speaking to you when you hear her (assuming for the sake of brevity that there is no time lapse between the speaking and hearing) and that she, in turn, hears your response and subsequently reacts to it, and so on back and forth. Each "moves" the other. This sort of intimate interaction cannot be achieved if you know that your correspondent timelessly knows everything you say in the course of the "conversation" and timelessly causes you to hear his "responses" at certain times, as would Helm's timeless God. Think, in this connection, of conversing over the phone with a tape recording that was made in advance by some prescient individual who knew just what you would say. Once you learn of this fact there no longer is any sense of intimacy between you and this being. The *Biblical* apparent direct perceptions of the presence of God are good examples of the sort of intimate dialogue that is so central to the working theist. Job would be very upset if he learned that he was "talking" with a tape recorded message.

21

Just as a personal God could *you* our *I*'s and thereby know differently personally indexed counterpart propositions to the ones we express by using "I," a temporal God can, at any given time, know different temporally indexed counterpart propositions to those that are truly expressible at earlier and later times. And since the former entail the latter, his failure to know every true A-proposition and personal indexical proposition is significantly lessened. For example, that S was F yesterday entails that yesterday S is then (that is, at that time) F. Through the entailment relations between the tensed propositions expressed by persons at different times, a sort of temporal "intimacy" is achieved across these times, but it is quite limited because a conversation could take place between differently temporally positioned persons only if causation, *per impossible*, could go backward.

There is yet another reason why a conversation requires that the communicants share the same temporal but not the same spatial perspective that rests on a very deep disanalogy between *here* and *now* with respect to the concept of objectivity, further undermining premise (i), the analogical premise, in the general form of the parody argument. After this disanalogy is unearthed, it will be employed in showing why there cannot be a conversation between a person existing now and one existing earlier than now whereas there can be a conversation between a person existing here and one existing in front of (to the rear of, etc.) here. The link between the concept of a conversation and that of objectivity is that a conversation requires that the communicants agree in their judgments of objectivity, that there is an objective reality that they share in common.

A determination is objective only if it is not subject to choice and is common to or agreed upon by other observers. *Now* satisfies these two requirements for objectivity but *here* satisfies neither. They are conceptually disanalogous in these respects in that the spatial (temporal) analogue to a given proposition containing a spatial (temporal) indexical term differs from it in its modal status, that is, its being necessary, contingent, or impossible. A spatial (or temporal) analogue to a given proposition is formed by replacing every spatial and temporal term in it, respectively, with a suitable temporal and spatial term. "Here" is to be replaced with "now" and "earlier than" by "in front of," though "to the rear, or right, or left of," would work equally well. Thus, the spatial analogue to the proposition that an object cannot now wholly occupy two different places is that an object cannot here wholly occupy two different times. This brings out a conceptual disanalogy between *here* and *now*, since the former is necessary and the latter impossible, which is due to the fact that an object has spatial but not temporal parts.

Whereas the use of *now* is not subject to selection or choice, the use of *here* is. This can be brought out clearly by the following pair of analogues.

(T1) A tokening of "now" now denotes a time but this very tokening could have denoted a time other than that time.

(S1) A tokening of "here" here denotes a place, but this very tokening could have denoted a place other than that place.

At first glance, there appears to be no disanalogy, since both (T1) and (S1) seem to be impossible.

But, far from being impossible, (S1) is necessary. The reason is that a tokening of "here" can be accompanied by an act of pointing and thus denote a different place than the one occupied by the speaker: I say to the movers, "Put the table here (as I point to a place in front of myself)." Since I could have pointed in a different direction than I in fact did, that very tokening of "here" could have denoted a different place than it in fact did. Obviously, there cannot be an analogous type of selectivity with the use of "now." Our only choice is when to token it, but once we have made that decision there is no further choice as to what time is denoted. But, with "here," even after I decide where to token it, I have a choice as to what place will be denoted by my tokening.

The response to this alleged selectivity-based disanalogy will be that a naked use of "here," one unaccompanied by any act of ostension, cannot refer to any place other than the one occupied by the speaker, thereby making (S1) impossible when restricted to naked uses of "here." The reply is that even with a naked use of "here" there is choice, for the speaker has chosen whether or not to use it nakedly. But, disanalogously, a use of "now" must be naked, and thus the speaker has no choice in the matter.

There is another respect in which "here" is selective and "now" is not. Even if a tokening of "here" were in no way selective, it still would be the case that

(S2) A tokening of "here" later than now could refer to both a place in front of here and to a place to the rear of here.

Whereas

(T2) A tokening of "now" in front of here could refer to both a time earlier than now and to a time later than now.

It is clear that (S2) is necessary, since it is possible for the speaker to be spatially free and rangy, and thus be able to change her spatial perspective at will in any direction in space. But (T2) is not necessary, because a speaker is not analogously able to change her temporal perspective at will in any direction in time. The reason is that it is impossible for a speaker who exists now to bring it about that a tokening of "now" denotes a time earlier than now, for causation cannot go backward in time although it can go in any direction in space.

The other, and more important, objectivity-involving disanalogy concerns the agreement-in-judgment-among-normal-observers test for the objectivity or veridicality of a perceptual experience. Whereas these relevant observers must be copresent with the perceptual experience, they need not occupy the same place as does the perceiver. This gives rise to the following conceptual disanalogy:

(T3) To test a perceptual claim made now, appeal is made to the noninferential perceptual claims only of observers who exist now.

(S3) To test a perceptual claim made here, appeal is made to the noninferential perceptual claims only of observers who exist here.

These propositions differ in their modal status since (T3) is necessary and (S3) is not. In testing the objective truth of a perceptual claim made here, we do not confine ourselves to the testimony of observers who are here, for someone who is not here can have just as good a view, often better, of what is happening here. But we do not elicit the noninferential perceptual judgments of past or future observers with regard to what exists or is happening now. Their testimony as to what they then noninferentially perceive is irrelevant. If we were able, *per impossible*, to converse with Plato we would not ask him what time it is now, for what he says after consulting his sun dial would be totally irrelevant.

We want those with whom we enter into intimate dialogue to share our view of objective reality, and thus they must be copresent with us and share temporal indexical perspectives of past, present and future. A timeless God could not have these perspectives and thus could not share our sense of objective reality. These perspectives are essential to our lives as agents in which we deliberate and intentionally carry out our decisions. If we want a God who is available to us as agents, a God who will warn, direct, and comfort us in our worldly endeavors, it cannot be the timelessly eternal God. But if, on the other hand, we want a God with whom to mystically commune, he would be the one that we want. Most theists want both gods and the challenge is to find a way to synthesize them, which again raises the issue of the doctrine of the Trinity. Additional reasons for placing God in time will be given in Chapter 3 when the free will defense is discussed.

SOVEREIGNTY

There are other divine attributes for which atheological arguments have not yet been constructed, in particular, sovereignty and omnibenevolence. God's sovereignty requires that he completely and solely determines *everything*. As was the case with omnipotence, it is necessary to restrict this everything to what it is logically consistent for him to determine. He doesn't determine his own existence, for example. A more controversial issue is whether he can determine necessary truths, such as that two and two are four, and that no proposition is both true and false.

Of special interest is whether he can determine moral truths concerning what is good and bad, right and wrong. Many theists have contended that God's sovereignty extends even to what counts as morally good and right. Ethical propositions acquire their truth-values (their truth or falsity) from Divine decisions or commands. The following sovereignty-benevolence atheological argument is directed against this being possible:

1. God determines the truth-values of ethical propositions. Divine Command Theory of Ethics

2. God is essentially benevolent. Tenet of theism

Taking God to be omnitemporally eternal, it is deduced from 2 that

3. God is benevolent prior to his decisions as to what truth-values ethical propositions will have.

But from 1 it follows that

4. Nothing is good or bad, right or wrong, prior to God's decision as to what truth-values ethical propositions will have.

But 4 contradicts 3.

One might try to escape this argument by conceiving of God's decisions as to what truth-values ethical propositions are to have as an abiding one that endures throughout an infinite past and future, so that there is no time prior to that at which he makes these decisions. This is not an ad hoc move, since God's immutability requires that he not change his mind from one time to another. The same result would be achieved if the theist were to conceive of God as timelessly eternal. Again, the consequence will be that here is no time at which God has not yet made his ethical decisions.

A different version of the sovereignty-benevolence argument must be deployed against these two ways of conceiving of God's ethical decisions as being immutable. An additional premise must be added, namely, that God must have a reason for any choice he makes that is based on some moral good that is realized by his choice. But this requires that there is something morally good that is prior in the order of explanation or determination, rather than time, to God's choice as to what truth-values ethical propositions will have in the sense that it helps to explain or determine God's choice in this matter. Thus, there both is and is not something that is good prior in the order of explanation or dependency to God's choice as to what is good. This, I take it, is the thrust of the argument of Plato's *Euthyphro* in which it is contended that the gods love something because it is pious rather than it being pious because the gods love it. And this seems right to me. Ethical propositions are not of the right categoreal sort to be made true by anyone's decision, even God's.

The purpose of the preceding atheological arguments is not to settle anything, surely not to disprove God's existence, but rather to loosen you up so that you realize that there still is a lot of work that needs to be done in developing an adequate conception of God's nature. One thing it should do is to free you from slavishly following past orthodoxy through the realization that there are serious problems with how the great medieval philosophers conceived of God's nature.

As this book proceeds you will again and again be confronted with this problem. The most important atheological argument, which does not have the friendly intent of getting the theist to improve her conception of God but rather to disprove God's existence, is the argument based on the existence of evil. So important and complex is the problem of evil that a special chapter, Chapter 3, is reserved for its discussion.

2

Epistemic Justifications of Belief

This chapter will critically examine the attempt to show that it is evidentially or epistemically rational to believe that God exists based on arguments for the existence of God. In addition to considering the important traditional arguments, some oddball arguments will be presented for your delectation and titillation. My favorite in this genre is one that a student of mine wrote down on an examination in answer to the question, "What is the strongest argument for the existence of God?" Answer: "God must exist; for if he didn't exist, how could he have created the world?" As Mister Rogers might say, "Can you say begging the question?" Hopefully, the arguments will improve as the chapter progresses.

Arguments for the existence of God come in different shapes and sizes. First, there is a distinction between a priori and a posteriori arguments. All of the premises of the former are knowable without appeal to sense experience, but the latter have at least one premise that is not so knowable. Then there is the distinction between deductive and inductive arguments. The former's conclusion is logically entailed by its premises—it's logically impossible for all of the premises to be true and its conclusion false—but this is not the case with the latter. These distinctions will become clear as we progress.

ONTOLOGICAL ARGUMENTS

There are many different versions of this argument. What they have in common is an attempt to *deduce* God's existence from a mere analysis of the concept of God. Furthermore, they are a priori arguments, because all of their premises are supposed to be knowable independently of sense experience. They are the darlings of theists who are enamored of the mathematical style of reasoning. In response to critics, such as Hume and the logical positivists, who deny that the existence of an individual can ever be deduced from an analysis of the concept of that individual, they could say that this is just what happens in mathematics when, for example, the existence of a number meeting certain conditions, such as being the square root of 9, is deduced from axioms, definitions, and postulates, all of which are knowable a priori. And, given that God resembles numbers in respect to not being in space or time, the possibility of deducing God's existence a priori must not be dismissed out of hand. In fact, an argument based on this similarity will be considered shortly.

Before getting down to the most important ontological arguments, a couple of interesting but less compelling versions will be considered. There is a probability–based version that conceives of God as being omnitemporally eternal, thus requiring that if he exists at any time he exists at every time without beginning or end. The key premise, which supposedly will be granted by the opponent of the argument, is that it is at least possible that God exists. Now, necessarily, whatever possibly exists in time exists at some time if there are infinitely many times, since each moment of time is an opportunity for it to exist. There are infinitely many times. Therefore, God exists at some time and thus at every time without beginning or end. One challenge to this argument is to prove that it is necessary that there are infinitely many times. If this premise is downgraded to the weaker claim that it is contingently true that there exist infinitely many moments of time, the argument ceases to be a priori, but it still could be interesting in its own right. Another challenge is to show that by the same reasoning it can be shown that God does not exist by simply replacing the premise in the original argument that it is possible that God exists with the equally plausible premise that it is possible that God does not exist. Since there are infinitely many times, this possibility will be realized at some time. But since God exists at all times if he exists at any time, it follows that he does not exist.

The following more influential ontological argument was given by Duns Scotus and in recent times by James Ross.

1. It is impossible that anything would prevent God from existing. Conceptual truth

2. For any individual that either exists or fails to exist, it is possible that there is an explanation of its existing or failing to exist. Weak version of the principle of sufficient reason

3. God does not exist. Assumption for indirect proof

4. It is possible that there is an explanation for God's not existing. From 2 and 3

5. It is not possible that there is an explanation for God's not existing. From 1

6. It is possible that there is an explanation for God's not existing, and it is not possible that there is an explanation for God's not existing. From 4 and 5 by conjunction

7. It is not possible that God does not exist. From 3–6 by indirect proof

From the proposition that God does not exist, an explicit contradiction is deduced, thereby showing that it is impossible that God does not exist, which is equivalent to the proposition that it is necessary that God exists.

An attractive feature of this argument is that it manages to make do in premise 2 with a very weak version of the principle of sufficient reason that requires only that for every true existential proposition or its denial it is at least possible that there is an explanation, not that there actually is one. But in spite of this attractive feature, the argument might come up short, for it is questionable whether step 4 follows from premise 1. For this deduction to be valid, the only possible explanation for the nonexistence of God must be a causal one in terms of something that causally prevents God from existing. To begin with, it should be noted that, according to the ontological argument, the explanation for God's existence is not a causal one, being based on this argument. Why, then, should the explanation of his nonexistence have to be a causal one? Why couldn't it be based on some fact that logically, not causally, precludes his existence, such as that there are evils that are not justified and therefore cannot coexist with God. In this connection, think of other noncausal explanations for something being absent. The reason why I am not now in San Francisco is that I am now in Knoxville. The latter proposition, however, does not describe something that causes the former to be true. Rather, it reports a state of affairs that logically, not causally, precludes my being in San Francisco now in virtue of the conceptually necessary proposition that an object cannot simultaneous occupy two different places.

Saint Anselm is the *classicus locus* for ontological arguments. He gave several versions that are based on God being an abstract entity in the sense of not occupying space or time. Basically, they get down to this.

1. God is an abstract entity. Tenet of theism
2. Every abstract entity either necessarily exists or necessarily does not exist. Premise
3. Either God necessarily exists or God necessarily does not exist. From 1 and 2
4. It is possible that God exists. Premise
5. It is not the case that God necessarily does not exist. From 4
6. God necessarily exists. From 4 and 5 by disjunctive syllogism (Either *p* or *q*, not-*p*; therefore, *q*)

Just as Anselm's argument in Chapter 1 (that God must be timeless; for, if he were in time, he would have the possibility of ceasing to exist, which violates his being a greatest conceivable being) rested on a hasty generalization from ordinary temporal particulars, this argument rests on a hasty generalization from ordinary abstract entities, such as numbers and properties, that occupy Plato's heaven. It was seen that God is very different from these sorts of abstract entities in that he has a life and is a causal agent, and thus it shouldn't be assumed that what holds for Platonic-type abstract entities also holds for God. Furthermore, this argument can be challenged by a parallel argument that replaces its premise 4—that it is possible that God exists—with the equally plausible premise that it is possible that God does not exist.

Anselm's famous ontological argument begins with a conception of God as a being than which a greater cannot be conceived, that is, a being that essentially has every desirable attribute or perfection to an unlimited degree and thus essentially has omnipotence, omniscience, omnibenevolence, and the like. It does not matter whether this is how people ordinarily conceive of God. It can be a purely stipulative definition, for it is Anselm's aim to show that from this definition of God it can be deduced that he exists. The next step in his argument is to get his Biblical fool opponent, the one who denied in his heart that God exists, to grant that it is at least possible that there exists some being that instantiates or is an instance of this concept. From this admission of possibility, he deduces that it is necessary that the concept is instantiated by the use of an indirect proof in which a contradiction is deduced from the assumption that it is not instantiated, that is, that the being than which none greater can be conceived does not objectively exist. On the assumption that existence is a great-making property—that, all things being equal, a being is greater in a circumstance in which it exists than it is in one in which it does not—it follows that if that than which none greater can be conceived does not in fact exist, then it could be conceived to be greater than it is. And that's a contradiction, thereby showing that the assumption is not just false but necessarily false, and thus it is necessarily true that God exists.

Many objections have been raised over the years to this argument. One attempts to show that by the same reasoning it can be deduced that necessarily there exists a greatest conceivable devil, a being that essentially has all of God's omniperfections save for being omnimalevolent instead of omnibenevolent. This conclusion, moreover, is logically incompatible with the conclusion of Anselm's argument—that necessarily there exists a greatest conceivable being— since it is logically impossible for these two beings to coexist. The reason is that each being would have to be sovereign over everything, that is, be the complete and *sole* determiner of everything. Thus, there will be objects that are completely and solely determined by each of them. This argument for a greatest conceivable devil would be chal- lenged by Saint Thomas who argued that a being could not have one of the Divine omniperfections without having all of them, this being due to all of God's properties being one and the same.

Another objection questions whether it really is contradictory to say that, that than which none greater can be conceived could be conceived to be greater than it is. David Lewis has cogently argued that it is not. An individual, in addition to actually having certain properties, possibly has others which it does not in fact have. For each of the latter properties, there is a possible but nonactual world in which this individual exists and has this property. All of us have such properties, for in everyone's life there are unrealized possibilities, such as things that they might have done but didn't in fact do. You could have put more effort into getting a good grade in your calculus class but failed to do so. Thus, there is some possible world in which you do this and get a better grade, and, all other things being the same, you are greater in that world than you are in the actual world. Because the greatness of an individual can vary in this manner across worlds, we must specify which world is in question when we speak about the greatness of an individual. Superman, for example, realizes his greatest greatness in the Marvel comic book possible world but not in the actual world since he fails to exist in it and thus is at a significant disadvantage in fighting crime in the actual world.

The allegedly contradictory proposition—that the being than which a greater cannot be conceived could be conceived to be greater than it is—fails to be contradictory because it suffers from incompleteness since it fails to specify which world is in question. Is it the actual world or some other possible world? There is an implicit free variable or blank space after the final "greater than it is"; and, until it is filled in with the specification of some particular world, no proposition, that is, something that is true or false, gets expressed. Not all values for this variable result in a contradiction. To see why this is so, a perspicuous rendering must be given of the possibility premise. Lewis performs a great service to our understanding of Anselm's argument by giving a clear analysis of it in terms of possible worlds. To say that it is possible that there exists a being than which a greater cannot be conceived, which we will call a *maximally excellent being*, means that

1. There is some possible world, w, in which there exists a being, x, such that x has maximal excellence in w.

This being x realizes a greatness in world w that is not exceeded by the greatness of any being in any possible world. From 1 it cannot be deduced that w is the actual world, just as it cannot be deduced that the possible world in which you get an A grade in your calculus class is the actual world. And, if w is not the actual world, then it is true, *pace* Anselm, that this being, x, than which a greater cannot be conceived could be greater than it is, provided that the free variable that follows "greater than it is" is replaced by "in the actual world," given that existence is a perfection or great-making property. Thus, from the possibility that the concept of that than which none greater can be conceived can be instantiated, which is perspicuously formulated by 1, it does not follow that the concept is instantiated by some existent being, a being that exists in the actual world.

Contemporary ontological arguers, such as Hartshorne, Malcolm, and Plantinga, have attempted to find a way around Lewis's objection. The underlying insight of their new version is that the greatness of a being in some possible world depends not just on how goes it with that being in that world but also on how goes it with that being in other possible worlds, the possibilities or logical space that surrounds the individual. A set of china that is essentially unbreakable, that is, does not break in any possible world in which it exists, is greater than one that is just plain old unbreakable, that is, one that does not break in the actual world but does break in some possible world in which it exists. The requirement that a maximally excellent being must possess all of its omniperfections essentially takes note of this, since this assures that this being will be at its greatest greatness in every world in which it exists (which, unfortunately, does not entail that it exists in the actual world). The concept of God, accordingly, must get souped up so that a being than which none greater can be conceived be not just maximally excellent (essentially have all of the omniperfections) but also have necessary existence as well, in which a being has necessary existence if and only if it is necessary that it exists. Let us call a being who has both maximal excellence and necessary existence an *unsurpassably great being*.

From the admission that it is possible that there exists an unsurpassably great being, the actual existence of this being can be deduced. Although this new ontological argument is valid it faces the problem that, whereas the fool rightly was willing to grant that it is possible that the concept of a maximally excellent being be instantiated, he would have to be not just a fool but a complete schmuck to grant that it is possible that the concept of an unsurpassably great being be instantiated. For in granting that it is possible that there is an unsurpassably great being, he is granting that it is possible that it is necessary that there is a maximally excellent being. But if his consent to the latter is to be an informed one, he must know that the nested modal operators, "It is possible that it is necessary," is to be subject to the axiom of the S5 system of modal logic, according to which whatever is possibly necessary is necessary, that is, if it is possible that it is necessary that p, then it is necessary that p. This has the consequence that a proposition's modal status is world-invariant. Since it is possible that the proposition that it is necessary that there is a maximally excellent being, this proposition is true in some possible world. But given that a necessary proposition is true in every possible world, it follows that it is true in the actual world that there is a maximally excellent being. The fool is well within his rights to charge the S5-based ontological argument with begging the question in its possibility premise.

The intelligent S5 arguer, such as Plantinga, would grant that the argument does not succeed as a piece of natural theology, but then would point out that it nevertheless serves the purpose of showing that it is not irrational or epistemically impermissible to believe that God exists; for the argument is valid and has premises, including the possibility one, that are just as likely to be true as not.

If a stalemate of intuitions is to be overcome, the opponent of the argument must give some good argument for why its possibility premise is false. This could be done by finding some concept that intuitively seems to have more likelihood of being instantiatable than does the concept of being unsurpassably great and that is strongly incompatible with it in that if either concept is instantiated in any possible world, the other is instantiated in none. The concept could be that of being an unjustified evil, meaning an evil that God does not have a morally exonerating excuse for permitting. It is impossible that God coexists with such an evil. But since an unsurpassably great being, if it possibly exists, exists in every possible world, in no possible world is there an unjustified evil. But it certainly seems more likely that it is possible that there be an unjustified evil than that there be an unsurpassably great being. Even some theists seem to grant the possibility of an unjustified evil when they exercise themselves in constructing theodicies that attempt to show that the apparently unjustified evils of the world really have a justification. Thus, by souping up the concept of God in the way the S5 ontological arguer does, the foundation is laid for an ontological disproof of God, conceived of as an unsurpassably great being.

The property that clashes with being an unsurpassably great being could be being a world in which persons, of which there are many, always freely do what is morally wrong. This certainly seems possible, but if God necessarily exists, it turns out not to be. For God's essential omnibenevolence and omnipotence ensures that he will prevent this from happening. But, since he exists in every possible world, it will be realized in none and thus isn't possible.

CHAPTER 2

COSMOLOGICAL ARGUMENTS

Unlike the ontological argument, which appeals only to highly sophisticated philosophers of a mathematical bent of mind, cosmological and design arguments figure prominently in the argumentative support that everyday working theists give for their faith. The reason for this broad pastoral appeal is that these arguments begin with commonplace facts about the world and then, by appeal to principles that look plausible, establish the existence of a being who, while not shown to have all of God's essential properties, properties that God must have to exist, is at least a close cousin of the God of traditional Western theism.

A cosmological argument begins with a contingent existential fact. A contingent fact is a true proposition that has both the possibility of being true and the possibility of being false, in which possibility is understood in the broadly logical or conceptual sense, as it was in Chapter 1. By extension a, contingent being is one who has both the possibility of existing and the possibility of not existing, with a necessary being not having the possibility of not existing. It might be the fact that there exists a total aggregate of contingent beings (the universe), or maybe that there exists at least one contingent being, or that one object depends upon another for its existence or its being in motion. This existential fact is not normative since there need not be anything particularly valuable or desirable about it.

Next, it is demanded that there is an explanation or cause of this fact in the name of the Principle of Sufficient Reason (hereafter PSR), which is suitably tailored so that every fact of this kind actually has an explanation. This is followed by an explanatory argument to show that the only possible explanation for this fact is in terms of the intentional actions of a God-like being. Thus, a cosmological argument standardly has the following three components:

1. A contingent, nonnormative existential fact
2. A version of PSR that requires that every fact of this kind has an explanation
3. An explanatory argument to show that the only possible explanation of this fact is in terms of the intentional actions of a supernatural, God-like being.

With these preliminaries out of the way, we can begin our survey of the different types of cosmological arguments. Saint Thomas Aquinas presented Five Ways of proving the existence of God, the first three of which are versions of the cosmological argument. The First Way begins with the contingent fact that one object is simultaneously moved by another, the Second that one thing depends for its existence upon the causal efficacy of a contemporaneous being, and the Third that there exists a contingent being. These are commonplace observational facts that only a complete skeptic about our senses would want to challenge. The explanatory arguments in the First and Second Ways are based on the impossibility of there being, respectively, an infinite regress of objects simultaneously being moved by other objects or objects depending for their existence upon the simultaneous causal efficacy of another being. These regresses, therefore, must terminate with a being who is capable respectively of moving another object without itself being moved by another or causing the existence of something without itself being caused to exist. Thomas then identifies this first mover or cause with God on the basis of our common ways of speaking about God—"et hic dicimus Deum"—thereby papering over a serious gap problem, since his arguments do not establish that these beings have all of the essential divine attributes, in particular, omnibenevolence.

The intuition underlying Thomas's rejection of the possibility of an actual infinity of simultaneous movers or causers is far from obvious, especially since he did not think it impossible to have an actual past infinite regress of nonsimultaneous causes, as for example an actual infinite regress of past begetters. An attempt will be made to draw out his intuition in a way that gives some plausibility to it.

The causal relation in a series of simultaneous causes or movers involves transitivity in that if X simultaneously moves (causes) Y and Y simultaneously moves (causes) Z, then X moves (causes) Z. Nonsimultaneous causation is not transitive, since, even though you were begot by your parents and they in turn were begot by their parents, you were not begot by the latter.

One reason that might be given for the impossibility of an actual infinite regress of simultaneous causes or movers is that if there were such a regress, there would be no member of the regress that could be held to be morally responsible, a fit subject of either praise or blame, for the initial event or object in the regress. But this can't be the right reason, since not all causal explanations are forensic in the sense of giving an individual who is to be praised or blamed for the effect.

Maybe Thomas's underlying intuition can be fleshed out by considering these two examples. In one, a group of boys attempt to get into the movies free by having each boy point to the boy behind him as he enters the theatre and when the ticket taker stops the last boy in the group for the tickets he claims not to know who these other boys are. The last boy has to pay for himself but all the others get in free. Now suppose that the regress of boys pointing behind themselves to another boy is infinite. Plainly, the theater owner would not be happy with this arrangement, since he would never get paid, just as you would never succeed in cashing a check if it were covered by a bank account that in turn was covered by another and so on *ad infinitum*. A system of credit, like a succession of boys entering a theater, must terminate with some actual cash. A second example involves a train of cars that simultaneously push each other, such that the first car is simultaneous moved by a second, and the second by a third, and so on *ad infinitum*. If the regress of movers were infinite, there would be no explanation of where the oomph, the energy, the power to move, came from.

There is an implicit appeal to a version of the PSR to the effect that something cannot come out of nothing. This can be made clearer by considering a circle of causes. Thomas ruled this to be impossible for the same intuitive reason that he proscribed an infinite regress of simultaneous movers or causes. Imagine that you meet someone who looks like you would look in ten years. He claims to be your future self and to have traveled ten years backward in time in order to give you instructions on how to build a time machine. Subsequently, you build one and then travel ten years backward in time to inform your past self about how to build a time machine. The intuitive grounds for Thomas's rejection of the possibility of this closed causal loop is that it violates the PSR, for there is no answer to the question of from whence came the knowledge of how to build a time machine. Similarly, there is no answer to the question of from whence came the power to move an object or causally sustain its existence in the case of an infinite regress of simultaneous movers or causers.

The Third Way begins with the unexceptionable contingent existential fact that there now exists at least one contingent being, say a tree. Can some version of the PSR be employed so as to deduce that there exists a necessary being that causes the existence of this tree? A contingent being has the possibility of not being, and thus given an infinite number of times, either through an infinitely extended past or a past time interval that is comprised of an infinity of moments of time, this possibility will be realized at some past time. Each moment is like a roll of the dice, an opportunity for this possibility to be realized. The PSR tells us that something cannot come out of nothing, so there has to be a cause of this being's coming into existence at this past time. Therefore, something had to cause this being to come into being out of nothing. But why couldn't this cause be itself a contingent being and it, in turn, be caused to begin to exist by an even earlier contingent being, and so on ad infinitum? Thomas's answer as to why this regress of contingent beings is impossible seems to commit an egregious error. For he says that if there were to exist only contingent beings, then, since for each of them there is a past time at which it doesn't exist, there is a past time at which each one of them does not exist. And, if there ever were nothing, then, given the PSR, nothing would subsequently exist, which contradicts the patent existential fact that there now exists at least one contingent being. This argument seems to commit the same howler as is committed by inferring from the fact that for every woman there is a man that there is a man who is for every woman (talk about polygamy!). In logistical terms it is $(x)(\exists y)xRy \supset (\exists y)(x)xRy$. But it is hard to believe that a great philosopher committed so obvious a blunder. With a little charity and imagination something interesting can be made out of the Third Way, but shall not be attempted here.

The Kalam Cosmological Argument of the medieval Islamic philosophers, which has been defended in recent times by William Lane Craig, also invokes the impossibility of an infinite regress but in a different way than Thomas did in his first Two Ways. It selects as its contingent existential fact that there now exists a universe—an aggregate comprised of all contingent beings. It then argues that the universe must have begun to exist, for otherwise there would be an actual infinite series of past events or time, which is conceptually absurd. Since something cannot come out of nothing, there had to be a cause for the universe coming into being at some time a finite number of years ago. And this cause is identified with God, which again occasions the gap problem. Notice that the version of the PSR that is appealed to is restricted and thus a less vulnerable version of the PSR; for whereas the unrestricted version requires explanation for every thing that exists or fails to exist, the former requires an explanation only for a being's coming into existence.

Just why is it impossible for there to be an actual infinity of past events or times? The answer is not obvious. Thomas, for one, did not think it to be impossible. Two kinds of arguments have been given for its impossibility. First, there are descendants of Zeno's arguments. It is not possible actually to go through an infinite series of events, for before going through the last event of the series, one would already have to have gone through an infinite series; and before the second last event, one would already have to have traversed an infinite series, and so on: The task could never have got started. But if there was an actual infinity of past events, then our world has traversed an infinite set of events, which is impossible. This argument depends on an anthropocentric notion of "going through" a set. The universe does not go through a set of events in the sense of planning which to go through first, in order to get through the second, and so on.

The other kind of argument is based on Hilbert's hotel that has infinitely many rooms, numbered 1, 2, 3, and so on, and where even if all rooms are occupied, space can always be found for a new visitor by shifting the occupant of room 1 to room 2, moving room 2's occupant to room 3 and so on. The slogan outside the hotel would say: "Always full but always room for more," and the Kalam arguer takes this to be incoherent. Or consider an infinite series of events, again numbered 1, 2, 3, and so on. Then, the subseries consisting of the even-numbered events should have fewer events in it. But in fact it does not, as can be seen by writing the two series one on top of the other

1	2	3	4	5	6	7	...
2	4	6	8	10	12	14	...

and noting that each member of the top series corresponds precisely to each member of the bottom series. Hence, the series of even-numbered events is both smaller and not smaller than the upper series. These arguments against an actual infinity, however, are all based on a confusion between two notions of "bigger than." One notion is numerical: A set is bigger than another if it has a greater number of members. The other notion is in terms of part-to-whole relations: A whole is bigger than any proper part. When dealing with finite quantities, anything that is bigger in the part–to–whole sense is also bigger in the numerical sense. But this is not so in the case of infinite quantities. Although in the part–to–whole sense there are more people in the hotel after a new guest arrives and there are more members of the original series of events, in the numerical sense there are not. Indeed, mathematicians take the failure of the part–to–whole sense of "bigger than" to imply the numerical sense to be the defining feature of infinity.

Probably the most powerful of the traditional cosmological arguments, since it involves the least amount of conceptual baggage and controversial assumptions, is the one given by Samuel Clarke. Like the Kalam Argument it begins with the contingent existential fact that there now exists an aggregate of all the contingent beings there are, but unlike this argument it does not have to invoke any controversial claims about the impossibility of infinite aggregates. It demands an explanation for the existence of this universe on the basis of a more general version of the PSR than the one employed in the Kalam Argument, namely that there is an explanation for the existence of every contingent being, whether or not it ever comes into being. For explanatory purposes the universe itself counts as a contingent being, since it is an aggregate of all the contingent beings there are. It therefore must have a causal explainer. This cause cannot be a contingent being. For if a contingent were to be the cause, it would have to be a cause of every one of the aggregate's constituents. But since every contingent being is included in this aggregate, it would have to be a cause of itself, which is impossible. The cause, therefore, must be some individual outside the aggregate; and, since an impossible individual cannot cause anything, it must be a necessary being that serves as the causal explainer of the aggregate. This holds whether the aggregate contains a finite or infinite number of contingent beings. Even if there were to be, as is possible for Clarke, an infinite past succession of contingent beings, each causing the existence of its immediate successor, there still would need to be a cause of the entire infinite succession.

It is at this point that David Hume raises what is considered by many to be a decisive objection to Clarke's argument. He claims that for any aggregate, whether finite or infinite, if there is for each of its constituents an explanation, then thereby, there is an explanation for the entire aggregate. Thus, if there were to be an infinite past succession of contingent beings, each of which causally explains the existence of its immediate successor, there would be an explanation for the entire infinite aggregate, and thus no need to go outside it and invoke a necessary being as its cause. Hume's claim that explanation is in general agglomerative can be shown to be false. For it is possible for there to be a separate explanation for the existence of each constituent in an aggregate, say each part of an automobile, without there thereby being an explanation of the entire aggregate—the automobile. The explanation for the latter would be above and beyond these several separate explanations for the existence of its constituent parts, as for example one that invokes the assembling activity in a Detroit factory.

William Rowe has given a variant version of Clarke's argument. He chooses as his initial contingent existential fact that there exists at least one contingent being. This is the plaintive cry that one might hear in a coffee shop, "Why is there something rather than nothing?" to which, according to Sidney Morgenbesser, God's response is, "Look you guys, suppose I created nothing, you still wouldn't be happy." The point of Morgenbesser's witticism is that even if there were to be nothing, that is, no contingent beings, the PSR still would require that there be an explanation for this big negative fact. The PSR is an equal opportunity explainer, not giving a privileged status to positive reality. We ask "Why is there something rather than nothing?" simply because there happens to be something rather than nothing. The PSR requires there be an explanation for the contingent fact that there exists at least one contingent being. It cannot be given in terms of the causal efficacy of another contingent being, since this would result in a vicious circularity. Thus, it must be in terms of the causal efficacy of a necessary being.

This completes our brief survey of traditional cosmological arguments. It is now time to critically evaluate them. It was seen that each faced an unresolved gap problem consisting in its failure to show that the first cause, unmoved mover, or necessary being has all of the essential divine attributes. The most serious form that the gap problem takes concerns the moral qualities of this being. Herein the problem of evil has been appealed to by the likes of Hume to argue that probably it is not an all-good being but rather a morally indifferent being. As a bumper sticker I once saw said, "God does exist. He just doesn't want to get involved." To counter the challenge of evil it is necessary to construct theodicies for the known evils and give convincing design arguments, which is the topic of the next chapter.

The most vulnerable premise in these arguments is its PSR, whether in its universal or restricted form. It is imposing on the non-theist opponent of these arguments to ask him to grant that every true contingent proposition (or some restricted set of them) actually has an explanation, for this, in effect, is to grant that the universe is rational through and through. And this occupies almost as high an echelon in one's wish book as does the existence of God. Hume argued that we can conceive of an uncaused event; and, since whatever is conceivable is possible in reality, PSR is false. Bruce Reichenbach charges that Hume confuses epistemic with ontological conditions. To be sure, there is a distinction between what is conceivable and what could exist, the former concerning the epistemic and the latter the ontological order. Nevertheless, Reichenbach's rebuttal is far too facile, for it fails to face the fact that our only access to the ontological order is through the epistemic order. The only way that we humans can go about determining what has the possibility of existing is by appealing to what we can conceive to be possible. Such modal intuitions concerning what is possible are fallible; they are only *prima facie* acceptable, since they are subject to defeat by subsequent ratiocination. They are discussion beginners, not discussion enders. In philosophy we must go with what we ultimately can make intelligible to ourselves at the end of the day, after we have made our best philosophical efforts. What can the defender of the PSR say to get us to give up our prima facie Humean modal intuition? Plainly, the onus is on him, since it is he who uses the PSR as a premise in his cosmological argument.

The cosmological arguer might respond that if the PSR were false, then the universe would be irrational. But it is not rational to believe what is itself irrational. We'll leave it to the reader to respond to this sophism.

Here is another argument for PSR. Nothing can exist without a sufficient reason for its existence; for then it would have no connection with existence, and thus not exist. All that this argument shows is that if a being has no sufficient reason for its existence, it has no *rational* connection with existence, not that it has no connection at all. It still could be connected with existence in the sense of being a part of existence or instantiating the property of having existence.

Another way of supporting PSR is to show that it is pragmatically rational for an inquirer to believe it, since by believing that everything has an explanation the believer becomes a more ardent and dedicated inquirer and thus is more apt to find explanations than if he did not believe this. This pragmatic sense of rational concerns the benefits that accrue to the believer of the PSR proposition, as contrasted with the cognitive or epistemic sense of rational that concerns reasons directed toward supporting the truth of the proposition believed. Since cosmological arguments attempt to establish the cognitive rationality of believing that God exists, they cannot employ a premise that concerns only the pragmatic rationality of believing some proposition, such as the PSR; this would commit the fallacy of equivocation, since "rational" would be used in both the pragmatic and cognitive sense. In essence, it would be arguing that it is cognitively rational to believe a proposition *p* because it is pragmatically rational to believe some proposition q, from which p follows or which is needed for the deduction of p.

A more reasonable argument for the PSR is an inductive one based upon our numerous and ever increasing successes in explaining contingently true propositions. The problem with such an inductive argument is that there is a significant difference between the contingent events and objects within the universe which form its inductive sample and the universe as a whole. Thus, it is risky to infer that what holds for the former also holds for the latter.

Recently, Alexander Pruss and I have concocted a new version of Clarke's cosmological argument (which might be difficult for an undergraduate to follow) that manages to make do with the very weak Duns Scotus version of the PSR that requires only that for every contingently true proposition it is possible that it have an explanation, thereby making it more difficult for the argument's nontheist opponent to reject the PSR premise. Thus it is not required that the proposition reporting the existence of the universe comprised of all the contingent beings there are actually have an explanation, only that it is possible that it does.

Recall that what is possible is realized in some possible world. Thus, if it is possible that proposition p has an explanation, than there is some possible world in which it does have an explanation, that is, there is a possible world, w, such that w contains the propositions p and q and the further proposition that q explains p. Once our opponent has granted the following weak version of the PSR

> W-PSR. For every contingently true proposition, p, there is a possible world w that contains the propositions p, q, and that q explains p.

we are able to deduce from it the strong version of the PSR, namely,

> S-PSR. For every contingently true proposition, p, there is a proposition q and that q explains p.

in which a possible world is a maximal, compossible conjunction of abstract propositions. It is maximal because for every proposition, p, either p is one of its conjuncts or not-p is; and it is compossible in that all of its conjuncts could be true together. This deduction, which is due to Pruss, goes as follows:

1. For every contingently true proposition, p, there is a possible world w that contains the propositions p, q, and that q explains p. W-PSR

2. p is contingently true and there is no explanation of p. Assumption for indirect proof

3. There is a possible world w that contains the propositions (p and there is no explanation of p), q and that q explains (p and there is no explanation of p). From 1 and 2

4. In w q explains p. True because explanation distributes over a conjunction

5. In w proposition p both does and does not have an explanation.

6. It is not the case that p is contingently true and there is no explanation of p. From 2–5 by indirect proof

7. It is not the case for any proposition p that p is contingently true and there is no explanation of p. From 6

Once we have established by this deduction that there actually is an explanation for the existence of the universe, we show by a series of deductions, which cannot be gone into here, that it is in terms of the free intentional actions of a very intelligent and powerful necessarily existent supernatural being. It must be a necessary being since the universe contains all the contingent beings there are. Since this necessarily existent being freely creates the universe, our argument escapes Schopenhauer's objection to the cosmological argument as being like a taxicab that we hire and then dismiss when we have reached our destination. For the cosmological arguer begins by demanding, on the basis of the PSR, an explanation for a certain contingent existential fact but when he arrives at his desired destination, God, he dismisses the PSR because he does not require an explanation for the fact that God exists and causes the existence of this fact. Since our explainer is a necessary being, it is a self-explaining being in the sense that there is a successful ontological argument for its existence, even if we aren't smart enough to give it. And, since it *freely* causes the existence of the universe, it is a self-explaining action for a Libertarian theory of freedom, which is the theory favored by the theist. This theory holds that a free action is not causally determined and is brought about solely by the agent who does it. Thus, to say that an action was done freely thereby explains it.

Once our opponent realizes that W-PSR logically entails S-PSR, he might no longer grant us W-PSR, charging it with begging the question. Whether an argument begs the question is relative to the epistemic circumstances of its opponent *before* the argument is given, not after it has been given. But this response would not silence Graham Oppy, for he claims that once you understand W-PSR *properly*, you can see that it entails S-PSR; and S-PSR is something which non-theists have good reason to refuse to accept. Those non-theists who were willing to grant W-PSR before they heard the argument which Gale and Pruss give should then say that they didn't *fully* understand what it was to which they were giving assent. So Oppy argues. Herein Oppy is demanding that in order to have a *proper* or *full* understanding of a proposition one must know all of its deductive consequences; and, thus, if you believe *p* and *p* entails *q*, then you believe *q*. This demand is completely contrived and has the unwanted consequence that every valid deductive argument, when its premises are *fully* understood, can rightly be charged with begging the question.

Although Oppy's demand is unacceptably strong, it still is true that to have an adequate understanding of a proposition one must know some of its entailment relationships. One would not understand, for example, the proposition that this is a material object unless one were prepared to deduce from it that it occupies space. But, plainly, one can understand that this is a material object without being aware of the very complex propositions that it entails within mereological theory about the logical relations between a whole and its parts.

We are not able to give a precise criterion for distinguishing between those entailment relations that are constitutive of understanding a given proposition and those that are not, since the concept of understanding is a pragmatic one and thus context-sensitive. But this does not mean that we cannot identify clear-cut cases of someone understanding a proposition and those in which he does not. And certainly one can understand a proposition that uses a modal concept, such as that of possibility and impossibility, without knowing every theorem of modal logic, just as one can understand a proposition employing geometrical concepts without knowing every theorem of geometry.

The most challenging objection to our argument has been given by Kevin Davey and Rob Clifton. Their strategy is to find a proposition that is strongly incompatible with W-PSR, in that if either is true in any possible world, the other is true in none, and which is at least as plausible a candidate for being logically possible as is W-PSR.

Their candidate for such a proposition is that there is a contingent proposition that lacks an explanation in the actual world, say that there are cats, or the universe for that matter. This modal intuition seems at first blush to have as much prima facie plausibility as does our modal intuition that every contingent proposition possibly has an explanation. But it turns out that these plausible modal intuitions are strongly incompatible. For W–PSR entails S–PSR and thus that in no possible world is there an unexplained contingent proposition, but the Davey–Clifton intuition entails that there is just such a world.

The strategy that we adopted for breaking this tie in modal intuitions was to show that one of the two rival modal intuitions coheres better with other of our background modal intuitions. To begin with, our belief in W–PSR coheres better with our proclivity to seek an explanation for any contingently true proposition. That we seek such an explanation shows that we do accept W–PSR, for we would not seek an explanation if we did not believe that it is at least logically possible that there is one. Second, we know what it is like to verify that a given proposition has an explanation, namely by discovering an explanation for it; but we do not know what it is like to verify that a given proposition does not have an explanation: There are just too many possible worlds for that to be accomplished. It is beside the point to respond that we know how to falsify the latter but not the former, since a proposition's truth-conditions are directly tied to its conditions of verification, not those for its falsification. These two considerations lend credence to the claim that, in the epistemic order, W–PSR is more deeply entrenched than is the Davey–Clifton claim that it is possible that a given contingent proposition has no explanation. From this conclusion it is reasonable to infer that, in the logical or conceptual order, W–PSR is a better candidate than is the Davey–Clifton proposition for being possible. All this, of course, is highly controversial.

TELEOLOGICAL ARGUMENTS

A teleological or design argument begins with a contingent existential fact that is valuable or desirable, differing thereby from the cosmological argument, whose beginning contingent fact does not have any normative status. It could be that there are purposeful natural objects, such as organisms, widespread law-like regularity and simplicity, the fine tuning of the physical constants of the laws of nature that makes life possible, natural beauty, apparent miracles, and the evolution of conscious beings possessed of rationality, freedom, and conscience. Next, it is argued, not that the only possible explanation for this fact is a theist type one, as is the case with the cosmological argument, but only that it is the best or most likely explanation. Herein some appeal is made to a principle of inductive, analogical, probabilistic, or abductive reasoning (inference to the best explanation), which takes the place of the need to appeal to PSR, as does the cosmological argument.

There are two types of teleological arguments, analogical and probabilistic. The general form of the analogical type is:

(i) Some natural object or process, O, resembles human artifact, A, in that both O and A have properties $P_1 \ldots P_n$;

(ii) A has the additional property of having a designer–creator as its cause. Therefore, it is probable by the rules of analogical reasoning that

(iii) B also has the property of having a designer–creator as its cause.

For the argument to succeed, the respects in which O and A are analogous must be relevant to O's having the additional property of having a designer–creator as its cause, and there must not be any disanalogies between O and A that would undermine the inference. For example, if O is a rock that has the same shape, size, color, and weight as a VCR, it would not be plausible to infer that it has a similar cause to that of a VCR. An example of a devastating disanalogy is a teleological argument based on an analogy between the universe as a whole and a machine, which holds that they both involve a concatenation of parts that work together harmoniously to realize some purpose or function. The damning disanalogy is that, whereas a machine functions within an environment in which it makes changes, the universe does not; for the universe is the totality and thus has no environment. Furthermore, it is highly problematic whether the universe has any function or purpose. More promising analogies are between artifacts and natural objects like organisms and their organs, say between a telescope and the eye or between a computer and a brain.

To avoid the charge of begging the question, the analogical premise in a design argument that reports the existence of some natural object or process that displays design or purpose must not be taken in such a way that it immediately entails that there exists a designer or purposer, for that would bring on a justified charge of begging the question from the opponent of the argument. Rather it must be taken to mean that there exists a natural object or process that has an *apparent* design, purpose or function, leaving it an open question as to what sort of a cause, if any, there is of this apparent design.

One objection to such organism-based teleological arguments is that we observe organisms being produced by other organisms of the same kind, and thus there is no need to invoke an intelligent designer of them. Sex alone can do the job. Furthermore, there is no absurdity in there being an actual past infinite regress of such begatting organisms. The reply to this is that what is explained by these facts about sexual reproduction is the mere existence of any given organism but not how it acquired its apparent design and purposeful behavior. And these facts go unexplained even if we invoke an actual past infinite regress of them.

David Hume, who is the most prominent critic of the analogical teleological argument, employed a number of strategies to undermine it. One is the use of a parody argument that presses the analogy in a way that yields a conclusion incompatible with theism: Since complex human artifacts, a building say, often have several creators who are material beings that usually do not outlive their creations, so it is with organisms. Just as we have Graziano and Sons as the designer-creators of a building, we'll have God and Sons. There is a counter to this objection. It won't do to say that one of the creators of an ape, for example, is the eyeball man, another the kidney man, and so on. For the ape lives in and through a complex environment, and thus there seems to be a need for invoking some master planner of the whole operation. Furthermore, all things being equal, we should prefer the simpler explanation, the one that does not multiply entities beyond necessity, which plainly favors the single designer-creator hypothesis. I leave it to you to figure out a strategy for responding to the parodies that wind up with a physical designer-creator who grows old and dies.

Another Humean strategy highlights a supposedly damning disanalogy: What is essential to inferring the designer of things like watches and houses in step (ii) of the teleological argument is that we have *seen* things of this sort, with this kind of complexity and on this scale, made by human beings; whereas, we have not seen anything comparable with respect to natural objects. We are warranted in inferring that the watch found on the heath is designed, to use Paley's example, because it is the kind of an object that we know from our past experience has a designer as its cause. But our past experience attests to there not being a designer for an eye or an organism, since we observe them coming into being from purely natural causes, such as vegetative or biological ones.

Hume's objection has been refined and extended in recent years by Antony Flew, who contends that the premises of a teleological argument, rather than supporting its conclusion, undermine it. For what these premises report is the existence of natural objects—nonartifacts—that display design and purpose that do not arise from any observed machinations by a designer-creator. This should count as evidence for objects displaying design and purpose without there being any intelligent designer or purposer. It shows that objects have a natural tendency or disposition to behave in ways that show purpose and design, being a case of, in the words of Irving Berlin, doing what comes naturally. Flew's objection can be deployed against every teleological argument. For example, if it is based on the law-like behavior of natural objects, it could be claimed that our experience shows that it is in the nature of these objects to so behave, and thus there is no need to invoke the actions of a transcendent supernatural agent to explain this.

But the most powerful blow against teleological arguments based on analogies between organisms and artifacts was not struck by Hume but by Charles Darwin who argued that these organisms were generated by the natural process of organisms mutating and only the fitter ones survived to reproduce. A teleological argument can be challenged by showing the existence of a satisfactory explanation of the items in question by a non-designed natural process, since that would challenge the claim that the theistic explanation is the only or the best one available. It might well be that *both* a theistic and a naturalistic explanation are true, but in the presence of a naturalistic one, the theistic one may not be needed or may not be the best one.

The impact of Darwin was to make teleological arguers regroup and switch to the probability-based version of the teleological argument in which it is argued that the naturalistic explanations, such as Darwin's, of the natural objects and processes upon which the old analogical versions of the teleological argument were based are highly *improbable*. The theistic explanation is to be preferred because it is more probable than that these natural objects arose through mere chance. It will not do to explain the existence of a watch by saying that the molecules making it up randomly came together under the influence of quantum randomness, because this process would be ridiculously improbable. However, the Darwinian claim is that mutation plus natural selection makes the existence of complex biological mechanisms probable. Is this true?

The new breed of teleological arguers would point out that, in the first place, evolution does nothing to explain why there were living organisms on earth in the first place. Evolution only functions when a self-reproducing entity is on the scene: It cannot explain the coming-to-be of such entities. And *prima facie* we would expect that any self-reproducing organism would have a certain minimal complexity. The simplest independent living organism we know of is the *Mycoplasma genitalium*, whose genetic code comprises 517 genes, with the DNA consisting of about 193,000 codons, each of which can code for one of twenty amino acids. Experiments suggest that only about 265–350 of the genes are needed for life. But even the 265 shortest genes would have a total length of 4239 codons. Since each codon codes for one of twenty amino acids, this gives us $20^{4239} \approx 10^{5515}$ possible DNA sequences of this length, and the chance that a random DNA sequence of the appropriate length would be equivalent to the particular sequence of one *Mycoplasma genitalium* organism is thus less than one in 10^{5515}.

An event whose probability is less than 10^{100} is astronomically improbable since it would not be likely to have been generated in the 12–18 billion years our universe has been around even if each of the molecules in the universe, there being no more than about 10^{80} of them, tried to randomly produce the event a hundred times a second. In practice, other DNA sequences could produce an organism with the same functional properties, there are many other organisms than this *Mycoplasma* that would be sufficient to start life, and there are scenarios for the start of life that do not involve a full-blown independent DNA-based organism coming about at random, so the actual probability is higher than one in 10^{5515}. However, the number gives one some idea of how difficult the life-production task is. We still do not have a reasonably probable scientific explanation for the origin of life.

Secondly, in a surprising development, there are scientists and mathematicians, most notably Michael Behe and William Dembski, who question whether Darwinian evolution can account for all biological mechanisms. Behe argues that, whatever the plausibility of Darwinianism may have been for explaining macroscopic features of organisms, on the microscopic level we find biochemical complexity of such a degree that it could not be expected to come about through natural selection. The problem is that there are *irreducible complexities*—systems which only benefit the organism once *all* the parts are properly installed. A system having irreducible complexity cannot be expected to evolve gradually step-by-step through natural selection. Behe has argued that the cilia of bacteria, our immune system and the blood-clotting system exhibit irreducible complexity. Findings like this have been challenged and evolutionary mechanisms for at least some of these systems have been proposed. At the moment, this dispute is not resolvable, and we must await future scientific breakthroughs.

Instead of focusing on biological detail, many modern teleological arguers who give the probability-based version prefer to point to the apparent fact that the laws of nature, and the various constants in them, are precisely such as to allow for life. For instance, the universal law of gravitation states that the force between two masses is equal to G times the product of the masses divided by the square of the distance, where G is the gravitational constant equal approximately to 6.672×10^{-11} in the metric system. But although this constant could, *prima facie*, have any other real number as its value, only a narrow range of values of that constant would allow for, say, the formation of apparent prerequisites for life, such as stars. Likewise, it is claimed that, were the laws of nature themselves somewhat different, life could not form.

Of course, it could be that the progress of science will unify all the laws of nature in a way that exactly predicts the values of the constants, and in a way that will make it seem "natural" that the laws and constants are as they are. However, this has not been done yet, and we can only go by what we have right now. It is claimed that, right now, our only good putative explanation of the laws and constants is design.

Gilbert Fulmer has replied that the discussions of the fine-tuning of the constants in the laws of nature all presuppose that we are working in a range of values similar to those that actually obtain or at least that we are working with laws of nature generally like ours. But how do we know that once we look at the totality of all possible laws of nature and constants therein, we might not find that the majority of these are compatible with life, albeit perhaps life of a significantly different sort than we find here. In reply to this kind of an argument, John Leslie has used the analogy of a wasp on a wall. Imagine we see that a wasp on a wall was hit by a dart. Around the wasp, there is a large clear area with no wasps. We are justified in inferring that someone *aimed* the dart at the wasp even if there are lots of wasps further away on the wall. To infer design, one does not need the paucity of fine-tuned universes *simpliciter*, but simply in our local area. Besides, we do have good reason to think that if we look at all possible universes, it is not the case that the majority of them can support life.

Finally, the many universes anthropic principle (MUAP) can be brought in. This principle states that there exist infinitely many universes, either sequentially or simultaneously, and thus it is not improbable that some of them would contain observers, while evidently we can only observe a universe that can contain observers. The MUAP claims that, in general, we have no right to be surprised to observe a feature of the universe necessary for the production of intelligent life, since it is likely that at least one of the infinitely many universes would contain that feature, and we cannot observe any other. Thus, perhaps, there are infinitely many universes, and hence we would expect that at least one would exhibit the kind of fine-tuning that makes life possible, and obviously we couldn't observe any other.

There are two forms the MUAP takes. First, it might be that, necessarily, for every logically possible universe there exists a concrete universe that instantiates it or is its actualization. This runs into a multitude of paradoxes. To begin with, it undercuts inductive reasoning. Suppose God phoned you and, after having assured you with sufficiently impressive miracles that he is God, told you that he created at least as many universes with the same past as yours in which gravity fails to hold tomorrow as ones in which gravity continues tomorrow, but neglected to tell you which kind of universe he put you in. By standard canons of reasoning, you would be rationally required to assign at least as great epistemic probability to the claim that gravity will hold tomorrow as to the claim that it will not. Therefore, your inductive inference that tomorrow gravity will hold as it has always held would be undercut. But this form of the MUAP is just like this call from God: It tells us that every logically possible world is instantiated by some concrete universes, and certainly then there will be at least as many universes which have the same past as this world in which gravity will fail to hold tomorrow as ones where gravity will continue as before. Since this form of the MUAP undercuts induction, it should be rejected.

Alternately, it could be that all or infinitely many universes exist satisfying the same *basic* laws of nature, albeit with different constants in them. It does not matter here whether these universes exist simultaneously or sequentially. This version of MUAP, however, fails to block the question of why *these* basic laws of nature hold rather than others. It might, after all, be that the vast majority of possible sets of laws of nature could not support intelligent enmattered life because the vast majority would involve massive irregularity.

It is worth noting parenthetically that a multiple-universe theory has also been used to neutralize the argument against theism from evil. Donald Turner proposes that a perfectly good God would create all universes that are sufficiently good, i.e., which it is better to create than not to. As long as our universe is above that cutoff line, God was justified in creating it, even though superior universes abound, for to create our universe and the superior ones is better than just creating the superior ones. Thus, multiple universes can just as much be used in defense of theism as in defense of atheism.

Another kind of teleological argument, which has been promoted by Richard Swinburne, is based on the fact that the universe displays widespread law-like regularity and simplicity. It is argued that there are only two possible explanations for a fact, those being either a scientific explanation in terms of boundary conditions and laws of nature or a personalistic explanation in terms of the intentional activity of an agent. Now, because a scientific explanation explains facts by invoking laws of nature, it cannot explain why there *are* laws of nature on the pain of circularity. Thus, if there is an explanation, it must be one that is given in terms of the intentional activity of a designer.

Several replies are available here. The first is simply to deny the call for explanation. The basic laws of nature are rock-bottom, and they have no explanation; it's just a case of things doing what comes naturally, as Antony Flew would have it. This approach is particularly attractive if one is willing to bite the bullet and accept the implausible claim that the actual laws of nature are logically necessary. Once one admits, however, that the laws are contingent, one faces the teleological arguer's claim that it is vastly improbable that things should behave in a regular way. This claim, however, cannot be based on observed frequencies, since we experience only one universe. And even if it could be shown by an a priori analysis that there are more disorderly possible universes than there are orderly ones, there would be no grounds on which it could be determined for any one of the infinitely many universes what is its probability of becoming actual.

Another objection to the Swinburne argument is based on MUAP, which posits infinitely many universes, and points out that there is a selection effect: We can only observe a universe that has observers in it. Now, a universe which for the most part displays causal regularity is a necessary prerequisite for there to exist finite knowers and agents, since empirical knowledge depends on identifying persisting objects. If so, then we have no right to be surprised at the order in the universe, given a many–universes theory.

Swinburne attacks the MUAP reply to his argument by noting that it is at most order in the past and even then only in our local neighborhood that is required for knowers and observers. Thus, even if there are many universes and we preselect for those that contain observers, nonetheless, by appeal to inductive reasoning, we should still find future order, and order outside our local neighborhood, to be quite improbable.

The probability version of the teleological argument has reached a new level of sophistication in Swinburne's book, *The Existence of God*. Herein a cumulative case is made for it being probable that God exists based on an agglomeration of the premises of all the many probabilistic arguments: That there is a world at all, that it displays widespread law-like uniformity and simplicity in its governing laws and theories, that there exist organisms and—in particular—conscious ones, that men have great opportunities for freely cooperating in gaining knowledge and shaping the universe, and that history displays certain meaningful patterns, including the apparent existence of miracles. This counters the divide–and–conquer strategy of the atheist who considers each theistic argument in isolation and shows that alone it doesn't amount to very much.

For each of the above arguments a Bayesian-based case is made out that the evidence appealed to in its premises makes it more likely than otherwise that God exists, which he calls a good "C-inductive argument." Using P for probability, h to stand for the proposition that the God of traditional theism exists, e for the empirical evidence contained in the premise of the argument, and k for background knowledge, the claim is that, for each of these arguments, the empirical evidence, e, that it appeals to is such that $P(h/e \text{ and } k) > P(h/k)$. The evidence, e, raises the probability that God exists over what it is relative to our background knowledge, k, alone.

After he has completed this task, the reader wonders what will result when the empirical premises of all these arguments are agglomerated. Let us call the resulting argument the "cumulative probabilistic argument." The question is whether it renders h more likely to be true than not. Using e to stand for the conjunction of all these premises, the question is whether $P(h/e \text{ and } k) > 1/2$. The response should be, "Who knows?" Since each of the arguments is a

C-inductive argument, it is only comparative; and because each fails to assign any numerical value to the probability of h, there is no procedure for determining what happens when we add them together. Mush added to mush gives mush. There can be several good C-inductive arguments for a proposition *p*, which together do not bestow a probability of greater than 1/2 upon *p*. It will be seen in the next section of this chapter that Swinburne's purpose in concocting the agglomerative argument is not to establish that the probability that God exists is greater than ½ but instead to bolster his argument from religious experience for God's existence.

Finally, it should be noted that all teleological arguments face the same kind of gap problem as infect cosmological ones. Just as there is a gap between being a first cause and being God, there is a gap between being a very powerful and intelligent designer and being God. The most serious part of the gap concerns the goodness of the designer, due to the fact that there is a lot of apparently unjustified evil, namely evil which would seem to preclude or render improbable the existence of God because no morally exonerating excuse exists for permitting it. To close the gap, the teleological arguer, like the cosmological arguer, must find a way of neutralizing the problem of evil, which is the topic of the next chapter. Herein we see the need to do the philosophy of religion in a global manner.

RELIGIOUS EXPERIENCE ARGUMENTS

It is not uncommon for people in very different societies and ages to have experiences they take to be direct, nonsensory perceptions of God. Are these experiences cognitive, a basis on which knowledge is gained of an objective reality that transcends the world accessed through the ordinary five senses? No doubt they have an overpowering noetic phenomenological quality that leaves their subjects sweating with conviction that they are. But appearing noetic and actually being noetic do not always coincide, as witnessed by the equally overwhelming noetic quality possessed by various noncognitive experiences, such as dreams and drug-induced experiences. Plainly, arguments are needed to support the cognitivity claim. Fortunately, there has been no shortage of arguments in recent years to show that mystical experiences, understood as direct nonsensory perceptions of the presence of God, are cognitive. They will be critically evaluated.

Most of these recent arguments are based, explicitly or implicitly, on an analogy with sense experience, the generic version of which goes as follows:

1. Mystical experiences are analogous to sense experiences in cognitively relevant respects.

2. Sense experiences are cognitive.

3. Therefore, mystical experiences are cognitive.

Since sense experiences are taken by all but complete skeptics to be cognitive, if mystical experiences should prove to be sufficiently analogous to them, they should be accorded all the epistemic rights and privileges thereunto appertaining to sense experiences.

Analogical arguments vary with respect to how strong they take the analogy to be. The weakest is a version of language-game fideism, based on the greatest story ever told, that the language-game is played. But that both types of experience are included within an ongoing normative rule-governed linguistic practice is too thin an analogy to support the inference of 3 from 2. For there have been numerous language-games, such as witchcraft and astrology, that their participants took to be cognitive of an objective reality that plainly are not, given that their belief outputs clash with those of more deeply entrenched and well-supported language-games. Furthermore, there are language-games in which belief outputs are based on subjective experiential inputs, such as those for making avowals of pain on the basis of introspective experience. In these subjective language-games the experiential verb takes a cognate accusative, "I pain (or feel painfully)" being the perspicuous rendering of "I feel a pain," just as "I waltz" is of "I danced a waltz."

A language-game can count as cognitive only if it supplies checks and tests for distinguishing between its veridical and unveridical experiential inputs. Thus, the analogy between sense and mystical experiences can be supportive of the inference of 3 from 2 only if there are tests for distinguishing between veridical and unveridical mystical experiences. But they cannot be just any tests, for this would allow cultist type language-games, in which the only test is based on what the cult leader says, to count as cognitive. The tests must be sufficiently analogous to those for sense experience.

Among the analogical arguments that require analogous tests there is a distinction between the retail and wholesale versions. The former, which was advanced initially by William James in *The Varieties of Religious Experience* and more recently by Richard Swinburne, draws the analogy between individual sense and mystical experiences, whereas the latter, which has been championed by William Alston and William Wainwright, draws the analogy between the sense experience doxastic practice (SP) and the mystical experience doxastic practice (MP), in which a doxastic practice is a normative rule-governed social practice for forming existentially committed objective beliefs from a certain type of experiential input, subject to defeating overriders. This is the wholesale analogical argument:

4. The MP doxastic practice is analogous to the SP doxastic practice in cognitively relevant respects.

5. The SP doxastic practice is reliable in that most of its belief outputs are true.

6. Therefore, the MP doxastic practice also is reliable.

Both doxastic practices are based on an a priori framework-constituting rule that holds the occurrence of the experiential input in question to constitute both evidence and a prima facie warrant for the belief that reality is the way in which it is represented in this experience. The rule is a priori because any justification of it will have to assume that experiences of this type usually are reliable, thereby falling prey to vicious epistemic circularity. The warrant for believing is only prima facie, because it is subject to defeat by overriders consisting in flunked tests. The wholesale version is superior to the retail one, since the needed tests must be part of a social practice, given that a rule requires the possibility of public enforcement, which is just what a doxastic practice supplies.

In Richard Swinburne's argument this rule takes the form of the "Principle of Credulity" (PC), according to which if it epistemically seems to a subject that *x* is present, then probably *x* is present, unless there are defeaters, in which an epistemic seeming serves as a basis for a subject to believe that the apparent object of the seeming exists and is as it seems to be. Since Swinburne gives full generality to PC, he does not have to present an analogical argument to justify extending it from sense to mystical experiences. His argument goes as follows:

7. It epistemically seems to the subjects of mystical experiences that God is present.

8. If it epistemically seems to a subject that x is present, then probably x is present, unless there are defeaters.

9. Therefore, God probably is present, unless there are defeaters.

Swinburne thinks that the only possible defeater for 9 is a powerful argument for the nonexistence of God, and it is the purpose of his agglomerative probabilistic argument for God's existence, which was discussed in the immediately preceding section of this chapter, to defeat this potential defeater.

My interpretation of Swinburne's argument as an analogical one, in which PC is initially applied to sense experience and then extended to mystical experiences on the grounds of their being analogous to sense experience, is a well-intentioned anachronistic interpretation of his text. For the unrestricted version of PC is not acceptable. A person's nonperceptual epistemic seemings are notoriously subject to all kinds of irrationalities. The best that can be said for a nonperceptual epistemic seeming that a proposition p is true is that it increases p's probability over its prior probability, but this watered down version of PC is too weak to enable Swinburne to infer 9 from 8. That it is pragmatically, as contrasted with epistemically, rational for subjects to trust their epistemic seemings is plausible, but this version of PC will not enable 9 to be derived from 8 but only

9'. It is pragmatically rational to believe that God probably is present, unless there are defeaters.

It now will be argued that the analogy between sense and mystical experiences is far too thin to support the inference of 6 from 5 in the wholesale version of the analogical argument. My argument is two-pronged: It is argued, first, that the tests for the veridicality of mystical experiences are not sufficiently analogous to those for sense experience and, second, that mystical experiences, on purely conceptual grounds, fail to qualify as perceptions and thus are radically disanalogous to sense experiences. In addition to rehashing some of my previously published criticisms, I will respond to objections that have been made to them and also will try to correct some blunders I made.

The major tests for the veridicality of sense experience include agreement among observers, successful predictions, and being caused-in-the-right-way by the apparent object of the experience. The agreement test requires the observers whose testimony counts as confirmatory or disconfirmatory of the veridicality of a person's sense experience to be normal and in the right sort of epistemic circumstances. With respect to the former, they must not be subject to any psychological disorder that would distort their perception and their sensory faculties must be functioning in a normal, healthy manner; and, with regard to the latter, they must be properly positioned in space and time and the causal chain linking the experience with its object be of the right sort.

The mystical analogue to this agreement test is woefully weak. In the first place, whereas there are objective, agreed-upon tests for determining when a person's sensory faculty is not functioning properly, there are no such tests for determining when a person's mystical faculty is not functioning properly. Furthermore, there is no mystical analogue to a sensory observer being properly positioned in space, since God does not stand in any spatial relations. That there is no mystical analogue to normality of observer and circumstances results in a pernicious evidential asymmetry in that the occurrence of mystical experiences are taken to be confirmatory but the failure to have them, even when the mystical way of meditating, fasting and the like is followed, is not taken as disconfirmatory. Thus the mystical agreement test is one that can be passed but not flunked and thus no test at all. It is like a heads I win, tails you lose sort of con game.

There is no mystical analogue to the caused-in-the-right-way test, because there are no supernatural causal chains or processes linking God with worldly events. Another disanalogy is that whereas we can determine on the basis of sense experience alone that a given sense experience is caused in the right way by its apparent object, we cannot determine on the basis of mystical experience alone that a given mystical experience is caused in the right way. Furthermore, the defenders of the cognitivity of mystical experiences cannot agree among themselves whether there are any limitations on what is the right way for God to cause a mystical experience. At one extreme there are those like Wayne Proudfoot who require that a veridical mystical experience be directly caused by God sans any worldly proximate cause. And, at the other extreme, there are those like Walter Stace and Houston Smith who allow for a veridical mystical experience not only to admit of a worldly cause but any worldly cause, even ingestion of LSD.

It is only the prediction test that seems to have any application to mystical experiences. All of the great mystical traditions have taken the subject's favorable spiritual and moral development and the beneficial consequences for his society to count as confirmatory of the veridicality of his mystical experience. They reason that if one is in direct experiential connect with God, no less realizing partial or complete unification with him, it should result in these favorable consequences. Thus, these good consequences are confirmatory of the experiences veridicality in virtue of categoreal link between them and God's omniperfections.

There are two difficulties with the mystical analogue to the prediction test. The less serious difficulty is that the predicted good consequences are just as likely to occur whether the mystical experience that is being tested is veridical or not, that is, the probability that that there will be these good consequences relative to background knowledge, k, and that the experience is veridical is about the same as it is relative to k alone, the reason being that k contains facts about the naturalistic causes and consequences of mystical experiences. No doubt, these good consequences are more likely to occur if the subject believes that his experience is veridical, but this gives only a pragmatic, not an epistemic, justification for him so believing. The more serious difficulty is posed by the existence of equally viable rival doxastic mystical practices within the great extant religions, with their different conceptions of what constitutes desirable moral and spiritual development, revealed truths that the experience must not contradict, and ecclesiastical authorities and past holy persons.

Another way that the prediction test is appealed to is that it is more probable that mystical experiences will occur if God exists than if he doesn't, that is, the probability that mystical experience will occur relative to the existence of God and background knowledge, k, is greater than the probability that mystical experiences will occur relative to k alone. But this is dubious, again, because k contains facts about the naturalistic causes of mystical experiences. This stands in stark contrast with sense experience, for which it unquestionably is the case that it is more probable that sense experiences will occur if there are physical objects than if there are not, assuming that k in this case contains neither that there are physical objects nor any evil demon-type hypothesis. What this shows is that a prediction test is confirmatory of the veridicality of an experience of an O-type object only if the existence of an O-type object has both explanatory value and prior probability with respect to O-type experiences. Mystical experiences of a God-type object have been seen to have neither. The theist might argue at this point that it is more probable that there will exist creatures of sufficient complexity to be subject to these causes if God exists than if he doesn't. This greatly complicates the case for the cognitivity of mystical experiences, but it might be, as Alston, Wainwright, Gellman, and Swinburne contend, that we must consider the global or agglomerative case for theism in determining whether mystical experiences are cognitive. If it could be established that God exists, this would greatly increase the probability that mystical experiences are reliable indicators of objective reality.

The defenders of the cognitivity thesis have ready responses to all of the preceding objections to the mystical analogues to the veridicality tests for sense experience. Both Alston and Wainwright stress that disanalogies between how these tests apply to sense and mystical experience are not damaging to their analogical argument if these differences are a result of a conceptual difference between the respective apparent objects of these experiences—physical objects and God. Because it is a conceptual truth that God is a completely free supernatural being whose behavior and linkage with the world is not nomically-based, the analogical arguer should not be bothered by the fact that the agreement and caused-in-the-right-way tests work in radically different ways for the two types of experience. But to show the conceptual basis for a disanalogy between them does not explain away the disanalogy, just as explaining why one has a disease does not eliminate the disease. Furthermore, a conceptually-based disanalogy is the most damaging sort there can be.

Alston contends that the disanalogy between the way in which the agreement test applies to sense and mystical experiences would be damaging if it resulted from an ad hoc requirement that this test can serve only as confirmatory for mystical experiences, thus being a test that can only be passed; whereas, it serves as both confirmatory and disconfirmatory for sense experience. Since the evidential asymmetry in the way in which the agreement test works for mystical experience results from the theistic creed, with its claim that God freely bestows grace on someone whom he permits to directly perceive him, no harm is done to the analogical premise. But, again, to explain why there is a disanalogy does not lessen the harm it does to the analogical premise.

I had argued that the challenge posed by religious diversity to the mystical prediction test is especially virulent: Because these rival mystical traditions have opposing consequentialist criteria of veridicality, they are more deeply divided than if they accepted the same criteria but differed with respect to how they applied to specific cases. In response, Alston wrote the following. "If there is no neutral procedures for settling the dispute, each party is in a better position to stick by its guns than they would be if there were such a procedure. This is because in the latter case the most reasonable course would be to suspend judgment until that procedure is deployed. In the other case, since there is nothing analogous to wait for, there isn't the same reason to deny the rationality of each contestant's holding firm." This shows only that when the disputants do not agree upon a decision procedure for settling their disagreement, each is pragmatically justified in holding firm in their rival beliefs. But Alston is supposed to show that each is epistemically justified in doing so. And herein the fact that they cannot agree upon a method for settling their difference more seriously divides them than would a disagreement about the facts, thereby discrediting the epistemic credentials of each of their claims. A better way for Alston to meet the challenge of religious diversity is to pursue the ecumenical route by showing that there are important commonalities between the mystical traditions of the great extant religions and that their differences do not amount to any incompatibility between their different reality-claims.

Another defensive strategy pursued by the analogical arguer is the divide-and-conquer one in which each of the preceding alleged disanalogies is discussed separately and shown not to be alone decisive. This is clearly seen in Wainwright's criticisms of my attack on the analogical premise. With regard to the agreement test, he contends that Gale *overstates* his case when he claims that there are no [mystical experience] analogues to the sense experience agreement test's requirement that the observer and circumstances be normal. No doubt, I am guilty of overstating my case, both here and elsewhere, given that before I entered philosophy I worked as a song plugger for a music publishing firm and became adept at the great art of the "hype-job." But, nevertheless, Wainwright does concede some force to my charge of disanalogy when he writes that the connection between the condition of the observer and him having an M-experience is admittedly *looser* than it is in the case of sense perception. Another example of his giving ground but denying that this alone is sufficient to wipe out the analogical argument is his claim that, admittedly, failures of agreement like these differ from those counting against the veridicality of an apparent sense perception. Even so, the evidential asymmetry Gale alludes to *isn't great enough* to make the mystical use of the agreement test look like a heads I win, tails you lose sort of con game.

The same is said in response to my charge that there is no mystical analogue to the caused-in-the-right-way test for sense experience. He writes that while these points are important, they aren't *sufficient* to *totally* undermine the caused-in-the-right-way test. For example, diversity [among different religions] is, as Gale says, a cognitively invidious disanalogy. Whether it is *sufficient* to destroy the relevant analogy is another matter. The tests, in general, aren't *as dissimilar* as Gale thinks. In response to another alleged disanalogy he counters that it is [not] *as devastating* as [Gale] thinks. And when Wainwright summarizes his discussion of the alleged disanalogies he concludes that the contents of the tests are not *totally* dissimilar although the disanalogies as well as analogies are striking.

The italicized parts of the text clearly bring out Wainwright's piecemeal, divide-and-conquer strategy for neutralizing the force of the disanalogies. Although he shows that each disanalogy is not alone sufficient to destroy the analogical argument, he fails to consider whether they are when agglomerated. Obviously, the issue of how close the analogy must be between the tests for the veridicality of sense and mystical experiences for the argument to work is a vague one; for, as my laid-back Canadian good old boy, Bob, who made a prominent appearance in my *On the Nature and Existence of God*, said, "Everything is just aboot like everything else." As I see the agglomerative case, Wainwright has unwittingly given away almost the entire family farm acre by acre, leaving him, at best, with only a tiny vegetable garden, to which Bob would counter that a vegetable garden is just about the same as a farm. I guess we'll always have Bob with us, damn him! But one thing is for sure: The agglomerative case is far stronger than one based on taking each disanalogy in isolation.

The same sort of divide-and-conquer strategy runs rampant in Alston's great, classic book, *Perceiving God*. He does grant that the unresolved problem of religious diversity does have *significant* adverse consequences for the epistemic status of CMP (Christian mystical doxastic practice) and other forms of the mystical doxastic practice (MP). But this candid admission of *significant* epistemic discreditation is counterbalanced by the claim that, although this diversity reduces somewhat the maximal degree of epistemic justification derivable from CMP, it leaves the practitioner sufficient prima facie justified in M-beliefs [mystical beliefs] that it is rational for him to hold those beliefs, in the absence of specific overriders. (Are these two claims logically compatible?!) Similar concessions of lessened epistemic cred-itability are made at many other places in his book in response to ways in which MP is SP's epistemic inferior. He admits that MP's agree-ment test is a pale shadow of SP's agreement test and shows that MP is epistemically inferior to SP" but it does not go so far as to show "that MP is unreliable." Other ways in which he concedes that MP is SP's epistemic inferior is that SP is far more well established than any version of MP, that everyone must participate in SP whereas only a small minority participate in MP and, moreover, have the option of not doing so. But, like Wainwright, he never considers whether he has given away the whole family farm acre by acre when all of his concessions are agglomerated. Again, we run up against Bob, and again it might well be that how one is impressed by the analogies and disanalogies depends on one's background belief concerning the overall case for theism.

Jerome Gellman's defensive strategy in his *Mystical Experience of God* also treads on this ineliminable vagueness but with a twist that brings his position perilously close to a language-game fideism with any old tests. He reasons as follows:

> There is no good reason to make physical-object claims our evidential standard.... Our ordinary physical-object beliefs are way overjustified by confirming evidence. We have extremely luxurious constellations of confirming networks there. Hence it does not follow that were mystical claims justified to a lesser degree than that, or not by similar procedures, that they would be *un*justified. All that follow would be that they enjoyed less justification than belief in physical-object statements, but perhaps be justified nevertheless.

Herein Gellman appears to be making epistemic warrant and justification internal to a doxastic practice, each being given carte blanche to determine the criteria for warranted or justified belief within its own practice. This relativization of warrant to a doxastic practice is language-game fideism.

The second prong of my attack on the analogical argument is to show that mystical experiences, on purely conceptual grounds, cannot be perceptual. That they are taken to be perceptual by their subjects doesn't settle the matter, since mystics can be mistaken in what they say about their experiences, as witnessed by their mistaken claim of ineffability. If they were ineffable, how come mystics keep writing about them and, moreover, do such a good job of describing their experiences, even for the straight community of nonmystics. Recall that we did not want to give mystics privileged authority as to whether their experience is noetic. That the apparent object of their experience is given independently of their will is consistent with their experiences not being perceptual: An experience of a pain has such a givenness but its apparent object is only a cognate accusative. What I hope to do is to unearth a conceptual truth about a perceptual experience that mystical experience fails to satisfy, thereby showing that

A. It is conceptually impossible to perceive God.

This would totally devastate the analogical premise. What follows is a reformulation of my argument in *On the Nature and Existence of God* (326–43) that I hope will escape the published objections that were made to it by Gellman, Plantinga, and Wainwright. Their objections are based on a misconstrual of the argument, but the fault is mine for not having more clearly formulated it, which fault I hope to rectify now.

The first step in my argument is to point out that it is a conceptual truth that

B. A type of experience can qualify as perceptual only if it is possible its object can (i) exist when not actually perceived, (ii) be the common object of different experiences, both by a single person at different times and by two persons at the same time, and (iii) be such that a distinction can be made between perceptions that are of numerically one and the same rather than qualitatively similar objects of that type.

It must be stressed that *B* gives only a necessary condition for an .experience being perceptual. There is no doubt that the object of a sense perception satisfies requirements (i)–(iii). But it is equally clear that the object of a mystical experience, also satisfies (i)–(iii). Requirement (i) is met with flying colors, since God is the most objective, independent type of being there could be, given his absolute aseity. Not only can (ii) and (iii) be satisfied, but we can have overwhelming empirical evidence that they are. Consider this possible course of experience. The heavens become completely dark across the world as a voice from above the clouds says, "I am the Lord thy God, and I assure you that these persons (or the same person at different times) had veridical mystical experiences of me. And, in case you doubt me, I will now bring about miracles M, N, and O," all of which immediately follow. To strengthen the case, we could imagine that the same message appears over the Internet and that there is lightning and snow that have the sign design of "I am the Lord..." This would make a believer out of me!

The sought for conceptual disanalogy, therefore, is not to be found in B but in the manner in which B's requirements must be satisfied. First, it will be shown how B is satisfied by sense perception and then it will be asked whether there is an analogous way in which mystical experience could satisfy B. With regard to sense perception, it is a necessary truth that the perceivers and the objects of their perceptions are housed in a common space-time receptacle in which these objects serve as the common cause, via the different causal chains that link them with these perceivers, of the, for the most part, law-like coherence among the contents of these perceptions. This receptacle account explains how objects can exist when not perceived by supplying the needed dimensions in which to house them, thereby satisfying (i). These objects are ultimately individuated by their position in this receptacle, it being a necessary truth that objects of the same kind cannot be spatio-temporally coincident. In order to perform this individuating function for these empirical objects, these dimensions of space and time must not themselves be empirically determined. The receptacle account also explains how (ii)'s requirement that an object can be perceived by more than one person by the different causal chains connecting it with these persons within the receptacle.

The receptacle account also satisfies requirement (iii). The receptacle creates the possibility of there being counterexamples to the principle of the identity of indiscernibles when restricted to fully general properties, a fully general property being one that admits of the possibility of multiple instantiations at different regions within the receptacle. And, as a consequence, we are able to distinguish between perceptions that are of numerically one and the same object and those of objects that are only qualitatively similar. In the latter case there are noncoincident objects that are hooked up with different perceptions via different causal chains.

Let us call the receptacle explanation of how requirements (i)–(iii) are satisfied a "dimensional explanation." So far it has been established that it is a necessary conceptual truth that

> C. For an experience to qualify as a sense perception it is required that a dimensional explanation can be given of how its object satisfies requirements (i)–(iii) of B.

It would be an egregious piece of linguistic imperialism to require that a mystical experience satisfy C if it is to count as perceptual. For the dimensional account in terms of the receptacle's dimensions invokes space, and the object of a mystical experience, God, is not in space. What must be done is to genericize C so that it is not required that the dimensions of the receptacle be those of space and time. They can be analogues of space and time that perform the same function that space and time do in explaining how (i)–(iii) are satisfied. This generized version is

> D. For an experience to qualify as a perception, it is required that a dimensional explanation or an analogue to a dimensional explanation can be given of how its object satisfies requirements (i)–(iii) of B.

I think it is pretty clear that there is no analogue to a dimensional explanation of how the object of a mystical experience satisfies (i)–(iii) of B. As a consequence, mystical experiences fail to be perceptual. And this is the demise of the argument from analogy.

It seems to me that the most reasonable way to challenge my argument is to deny that D is a necessary conceptual truth. Although it is obvious that sense perceptions satisfy D, it is not clear that all perceptual experiences must satisfy D. I am afraid that the best that I can say in response to this denial of the necessity of D is, "Isn't it?" It looks like I am again mired in the modal intuition bowl, in which opponents with rival modal intuitions go back and forth endlessly saying "Tis!" and "Tisn't!"

Even if my argument turns out not to be a "killer argument," as Plantinga characterized it tongue in cheek, it at least has the power to maim, for it significantly deepens the disanalogy between sense and mystical experience by showing that only the former has an object for which there could be a dimensional explanation or an analogue to a dimensional explanation of why its object satisfies requirements (i)–(iii) of B. It is yet another acre of the family farm that is given away by the analogical arguer; and, when it is added on to the other acres that have been given away as a result of there being only quite weak mystical analogues to the sensory tests for veridicality, the analogical premise is acceptable only by Bob.

Probably, I have overstated my case. It might well be that how compelling we find the analogy between sense and mystical experience is a result of how strong we think the overall case for theism is, which is an issue about which there can be widespread disagreement among equally intelligent and informed persons. Again, we see that issues in the philosophy of religion must be dealt with in a global manner.

3

The Problem of Evil

The greatest epistemic challenge to the rationality of theistic belief is based on the widespread existence of evil, much of which appears to be gratuitous or unjustified. There are two types of atheistic arguments from evil—the deductive and the evidential. The former is an atheological argument that attempts to deduce an explicit contradiction from there being both evil and a God who is omnipotent and omnibenevolent. The evidential argument, of which there are many different versions, uses the known evils of the world to infer the improbability of God's existence or the irrationality of theistic belief. Each will be discussed in turn.

DEDUCTIVE ARGUMENTS FROM EVIL

Before we get down to considering various atheistic arguments from evil, it is necessary to say something about what evil is and to distinguish between different types of evil. An evil is something which, taken by itself in isolation, is an ought-not-to-be, an "Oh, no!" Examples are physical and mental suffering by a sentient being, including lower animals, immoral action, bad character, and, a privation in which something fails to measure up to what it ought to be, such as a human being born blind. The qualification "taken by itself" is important, since some evils are not gratuitous because they are so-called blessings in disguise, being necessary for the realization of an outweighing good or prevention of an even greater evil. As members

70

of such a larger whole they are not an ought-not-to-be, although taken in themselves they are. A distinction that will play a crucial role in our discussion of evil is between justified and unjustified evils. An justified evil is one for which God, were he to exist, would not have a morally exonerating excuse for causing or permitting it. An evil can be both justified and gratuitous, as for example a merited punishment that is not necessary for the realization of an outweighing good or prevention of an even greater evil.

Another important distinction is between natural and moral evil, the latter, unlike the former, being attributable to the misuse of free will by finite creatures. Examples of natural evils are floods, earthquakes, typhoons, and famines. It is possible that we are mistaken in so classifying them, since, for all we can know with absolute certainty, they might result from the free evil doings of very powerful but finite creatures, such as the Devil or ETs, or some of them might have been prevented had we properly exercised our free will in discovering their causes and ways of preventing them. Some theists refuse to call anything but moral evil or wickedness an evil, thereby eliminating natural evils as challenges to theism. This linguistic maneuver, however, accomplishes nothing, for the problem still remains as to how God could be justified in permitting suffering that is not attributable to the misuse of free will by finite creatures. To accommodate this redefinition of "evil," natural evils could be called "schmevils," the problem now being how God could be justified in allowing there to be schmevils.

With these preliminaries out of the way, we can consider the deductive or atheological argument from evil as presented by J. L. Mackie, who is to be credited for being the first person to give an explicit mounting of this ages-old argument. The initial set of propositions is:

1. God is omnipotent;
2. God is omnibenevolent; and
3. Evil exists.

From 1 and 2 it is deduced that

4. Evil does not exist.

This yields the contradiction that

5. Evil exists and evil does not exist. From 3 and 4

Whereas certain Eastern religions would deny 3, Western theism cannot since it is based on the Bible, which abounds in descriptions of every imaginable type of evil.

It is plain that 4 does not follow immediately from 1 and 2. Some additional premises are needed and they must be either necessarily true or accepted by the theist. Mackie supplies the following two additional premises that are supposed to be necessarily true in virtue of linguistic rules:

> 6. An omnipotent being can bring about anything;

and

> 7. An omnibenevolent being prevents or eliminates every evil it can.

Clearly, these additional premises are neither necessary truths nor acceptable by the theist. In Chapter 1 it was seen that 6 must be restricted as follows:

> 6′. An omnipotent being can bring about anything that it is consistent for it to bring about.

And 7, in the light of the distinction between a justified and unjustified evil, must be restricted so as to yield:

> 7′. An omnibenevolent being prevents or eliminates every unjustified evil it can.

From the initial set of premises, in conjunction with 6′ and 7′, it can be deduced only that

> 4′. Unjustified evil does not exist.

but 4' is consistent with

> 4. Evil does not exist.

This manner of rebutting Mackie's argument, however, leaves us with the resident problem of explaining how a being who is both omnipotent and omnibenevolent possibly could be morally justified in bringing about or permitting an evil. What sort of a morally exonerating excuse could be available to this being, remembering that it is supposed to be God and thus omniscient and sovereign as well? The excuses that we are familiar with are applicable to human beings but do not seem applicable to God. The lack-of-power excuse for failing to eliminate or prevent an evil (I wasn't strong enough to lift the car that you were pinned under) cannot be available to an omnipotent being. And the excusable-ignorance excuse (How could I have known that saying "Niagara Falls" would send him into a homicidal rage) could not apply to an omniscient being. And since God is sovereign over everything he cannot be excused because of a lack of opportunity (I couldn't have saved him from dying from the rattler's bite because I did not have the needed anti-serum or I wasn't there). That no excuse that we know of seems applicable to God should worry the theist.

The theist could respond that it is unacceptably anthropomorphic to demand that at least some of the excuses that apply to us as human beings are applicable to God; for he is infinite and we are finite. This is the message of the *Book of Job*, about which a lot more will be said later in this chapter. This raises the problem from Chapter 1 of what is required of a *personal* God and just how anthropomorphic our conception of this God should be. Be that as it may, it would help the cause of theism if we could at least spell out some excuse that it is at least logically possible for God to have. To do this is to create a *defense*, which is a description of a possible world containing both God and evil and thus a world in which God has a morally exonerating excuse for permitting this evil. A *theodicy* is a defense plus an argument to show that this exonerating condition or possible world actually obtains or at least that it is not implausible in the light of what we know that it does.

There is the compensation-in-an-afterlife defense for God permitting or even causing an evil, regardless of how horrendous it is. It is not enough that God awards the sufferer with heavenly pleasures that far outweigh the suffering underwent by the creature in this life, for this would not justify his allowing the suffering. Why not just create the pleasures sans the suffering? Why not plug everyone in to an ecstasy machine that would produce in them the greatest pleasurable state, say a combination of an orgasm and a mystical state? It is necessary that the evil is an intrinsic organic or aesthetic part of the pleasurable heavenly outcome so that the value of this outcome depends upon the earlier evil. For a compensation-in-an-afterlife defense to be effective it needs to spell out what this would be like. Furthermore, this defense, even when properly filled in, leaves a lot of work to be done if it is to be upgraded to a theodicy, since adequate evidence or arguments would have to be given for the existence of God, as well as an afterlife, no easy undertaking. An attempt will be made to come up with better defenses, ones that are based upon what obtains on this side of the vale.

FREE WILL DEFENSES

The free will defense (FWD) attempts to show how it is possible for God and moral evil to coexist by describing a possible world in which God is morally justified or exonerated for creating persons who freely go wrong. There are several different versions of it. The following is a generic brand FWD that captures what is common to them:

1. It is God's intention to create the best overall situation or the best world that he can. Intention premise

2. A world containing free persons who freely perform both right and wrong actions, but for the most part go right, is better than any possible world devoid of free persons. Normative premise

3. God cannot cause or determine in any way what a created person freely does. Incompatibilist premise

4. It is logically possible that God is contingently unable to create free persons who always go right. God–could–be–unlucky premise

What happens to premise 1, the intention premise, if, as seems reasonable, there is no uniquely best of all possible worlds in a way that is analogous to there not being a largest positive integer (a world with 1,001 happy egrets in it is better than one that contains only 1,000 happy egrets, and so on ad infinitum)? In that case God will create a world that is overall worth having and, moreover, one that is devoid of any unjustified evil. It has been brilliantly argued by Robert M. Adams that even if there were a uniquely best of all possible worlds, God would not be morally obligated to actualize it, since by actualizing less good creatures than he could have he is bestowing grace upon them, that is, bestowing a benefit without consideration of merit, and grace is recognized by the theist as a virtue of God. This seems plausible when confined to nonmoral goodness such as beauty, athletic ability, and the like, but is highly dubious if it is moral goodness that is in question. But one thing is for sure: There cannot be any morally unjustified evil in a world that God actualizes.

The incompatibilist premise, 3, requires that a free action be determined wholly by the agent and thus not by something external to the agent, such as prior causes or even the will of God, which can be explicitly formulated as

L. A free act is not sufficiently caused by anything external to the agent.

Without this premise the proponent of the FWD would have no response to the objection of the causal or theological compatibilist who contends that God could have determined that every created free person always freely goes right by either, respectively, a suitable determination of the initial state of the universe and the causal laws or simply willing in his own inimitable supernatural way that they do.

Each version of the FWD will tell a different story about how the God-could-be-unlucky premise, 4, could be realized, of how it is possible that God be frustrated in his endeavor to create a universe containing moral good (good that results from the use of creaturely free will) sans moral evil. According to the normative premise, 2, the value of free will is supposed to be so great that God is morally exonerated under such circumstances for creating the Mister Rogers-type persons—you know, the very same people who are good some times are bad some times.

We will begin our survey of different versions of the FWD by considering the one that was formulated by Alvin Plantinga, who has a very ingenious story to tell about how God could be unlucky. We know from L that God cannot both create free beings and determine what they freely do. What he must do, therefore, is to create persons who are free with respect to certain actions and then leave it up to them what they freely do. This requires that God does not instantiate or actualize *a possible free person* but rather what I will call *a diminished possible free person*. The former is a maximal and compossible set of abstract properties that could be instantiated by a single person and contains the property of being free with respect to at least one morally significant action, A, that is, the property of either freely doing A or freely refraining from doing A. You can think of it as a set of abstract propositions that completely describes the life of such a free person, everything that she does and undergoes. The set is compossible in that it admits of the logical possibility of coinstantiation by a single concrete individual, and it is maximal because for every property that could be possessed by a person either it or its complement is included in the set, the complement of the property P being non P.) Each possible free person contains *a diminished possible free person*, which is its largest proper subset of properties that is such that for any action A it neither includes or entails freely doing A nor includes or entails freely refraining from doing A, in which a property H includes or entails another property G just in case it is logically impossible that H be instantiated and G not be. The property of being red, for example, includes or entails the property of being colored since it is impossible for an object to be red but not be colored. A diminished possible free person is a "freedom-neutral" set of properties. Each property included in a set of properties could be freedom-neutral in that it does not entail for any action, A, freely doing A and yet the set as a whole not be, for the set could contain the properties (either freely doing A or freely refraining from doing A) and doing A. The conjunction of these two properties entails freely doing A.

For every possible free person containing the property of freely doing A there is a numerically distinct possible person that includes all of the same properties save for it's including freely refraining from doing A instead. Let us call such a pair of possible free persons an "incompatible pair." Whenever you freely perform an action you instantiate one member of such a pair to the exclusion of the other. For any incompatible pair God will be contingently unable to actualize one person in the pair. Let our specimen incompatible pair be P and P_1, who include all of the same properties save for P's including freely doing A and P_1's instead including freely refraining from doing A. The question is what would result if God were to instantiate DP. Would the concrete instantiator of this diminished person or set of freedom-neutral properties freely do A or freely refrain? Plainly, it must do one or the other, since it has the disjunctive property of either freely doing A or freely refraining from doing A. Thus, it is either true that

> F. If DP were instantiated, the instantiator would freely do A.

or true that

> F'. If DP were instantiated, the instantiator would freely refrain from doing A.

Let us call a subjunctive conditional whose antecedent reports the instantiation of a diminished possible free person and consequent the performance of a free action by the instantiated person a "free will subjunctive conditional," for short an "F-conditional." If F is true, then were God to instantiate DP, it would result in P being actualized; whereas, if F' is true, were God to actualize DP, it would result in P_1 being actualized. Since F and F' are logically incompatible, it follows that if F is true God is unable to actualize P_1, and if F' is true God is unable to actualize P. But necessarily one of them is true and therefore necessarily true that God cannot actualize P or cannot actualize P_1,.

This proof assumed that the law of conditional excluded middle holds for F-conditionals. Herein the necessarily true disjunction is formed not from the disjunction of an F-conditional with its negation, as is the case when the weaker law of excluded middle is applied, but from the disjunction of an F-conditional with an F-conditional containing the same antecedent and the denial of the former's consequent, as is the case above with the disjunction of F and F'. Plantinga gives an alternate proof that applies only the law of excluded middle to F-conditionals. It begins with what Plantinga calls "Lewis's lemma," which, when translated into my terminology, says that God can actualize a possible person P containing the property of freely doing A only if it is true that if God were to actualize its diminished person DP, the instantiator would freely do A. It next is claimed by appeal to the law of excluded middle that it is either true or false that F. If it is false, then, given Lewis's lemma, God cannot actualize P; and, if it is true, then he cannot actualize P_1.

At the outset let us confine ourselves to possible persons that include the property of being free with respect to only one action, such as persons P and P_1 above. What we establish then can be generalized to more complex possible persons. Any incompatible pair of such simplified persons is a Dr. Jeckyl and Mr. Hyde pair, the former being the one that contains the property of freely doing A (which we'll suppose is the morally right thing to do), the latter the property of freely refraining from doing A (which is the morally wrong thing to do). God might not be able to actualize P, the Dr. Jeckyl member of the pair, since F could be false. But what could be true for this particular Dr. Jeckyl and Mr. Hyde pair could be true for all of them. Every incompatible pair of this sort could be such that it is true that if

God were to instantiate the diminished possible person common to both, the instantiator would freely do the morally wrong alternative. Under such unfortunate circumstances, God can actualize only Hydes, and therefore will not attempt to instantiate any of these simple possible free persons, assuming that his brand of benevolence requires that there be a favorable balance of moral good over moral evil.

The result can be generalized so as to apply to more rich possible persons that contain the property of being free in respect to more than one action. It could still be the case for every such person that it is true that if God were to actualize its diminished person, the instantiator would freely go wrong with respect to at least one of these actions, which shows that it is possible that God cannot actualize a possible world in which all free persons always freely go right.

At this point Plantinga can complete his FWD by claiming that in the possible world in which the truth-values of the F-conditionals preclude God from actualizing any Dr. Jeckyls or, more generally, possible persons containing the property of always freely doing what is right, he is excused for creating persons who sometimes freely go wrong provided that for the most part they freely go right. This completes my rough sketch of Plantinga's FWD account of the possible world in which God is unlucky and thereby morally exonerated for allowing moral evil.

There are three salient theses in Plantinga's version of the FWD that must be stated explicitly, since they are challenged by other versions of the FWD, namely:

I. Every F-conditional has a contingent truth-value, that is, is contingently true or contingently false.

II. God knows the truth-value of all F-conditionals prior, either in the order of time or explanation, to his creative decision.

III. God does not determine the truth-values of F-conditionals.

Theses I and II together comprise the doctrine of God's "middle knowledge," about which a lot more will be said when we consider alternative versions of the FWD. Thesis III is required by the Libertarian incompatibilist premise L, since if God were to *both* determine the truth-value of an F-conditional and create the instantiator of its antecedent, he would be assuring that this created person freely does the action reported by the F-conditional's consequent, and, thus, *pace* what is said in the consequent, this action is not free.

And this is a contradiction since this action is both free and unfree. This contradiction is avoided by having God do only half the job, being the determiner of which *F*-conditionals get their antecedent actualized but not their truth-values.

If God does not determine the truth-values of the *F*-conditionals, who or what does? There is an answer to this that is implicit in the Platonic ontology employed in Plantinga's FWD. Since possible persons, including diminished possible persons, are sets of abstract properties, they exist in every possible world. Abstract entities have both essential and accidental properties. The number two has the property of being even in every possible world but has the property of being Igor's favorite number in only some. Our old friend, diminished possible person *DP*, being a set of properties, has the same essential properties in every possible world, such as containing the property of being free with respect to action *A*. However, it also has some accidental properties, among which is the following: containing the property of being-such-that-if-it-were-instantiated-its-instantiator-would-freely-do-*A*. In some worlds it has it and in others not. It is all right to call this funny property of *DP* a "dispositional property" provided we are clear that it is not a disposition of *DP* to freely perform *A* if instantiated (abstract entities, with the possible exception of God, cannot perform actions) but rather a disposition to have its instantiator freely do *A*.

But what, it will be asked, determines whether a diminished person has one of these funny dispositions? As they used to say in the Bronx, "Don't ask!" Here's where the regress of explanations hits the brick wall of brute, unexplainable contingency. There are no further elephants or tortoises upon whose back this contingency rests. Let us now consider some objections to Plantinga's FWD.

According to its Story of Creation the *F*-conditionals are God's kryptonite, limiting his power in a similar way to that in which fate limits the powers of the Greek gods. In both cases there is a force or power above and beyond the control of the individual that limits its powers to do what it wants. The idea that God must be lucky, that he must be dealt a favorable poker hand of *F*-conditional facts, if he is to be able to create a universe containing moral good sans moral evil, strikes some as blasphemous, as a radical distortion of the orthodox concept of God's omnipotence. While Plantinga's account of omnipotence is not every theist's cup of tea, certainly not that of the great medieval theists, it might be the cup of tea that will prove most digestible and healthy for theism in its effort to construct an adequate defense for God's permitting moral evil. Recall the moral of Chapter 1—that we should not allow ourselves to be intimidated by orthodoxy in designing the concept of God.

Numerous objections have been made to Plantinga's FWD, but each one admits of a response. The first claims, contra the normative premise, that it would be better for God to create a world containing conscious automata who are programmed by God always to go morally right than a world containing the Mister Rogers-type free persons. Plainly, this is not the normative intuition of the theist, who places a much greater value upon free will than does this objection. And since it is the internal consistency of theism that is challenged by the deductive argument from evil, it should be the theist's normative intuition that is operative. And, by the way, it is a normative intuition that is shared by numerous nontheists, some being willing to go so far as to hold that a world containing free creatures who go wrong for the most part is better than a world devoid of free creatures.

There are a number of objections of the "God-can-do-more" variety. One version maintains that God could ensure that all created free persons always freely go right by a selective use of his power of grace: For example, when Mayor Curley is deliberating about whether or not to accept a bribe, God could cause Curley to have conscious experiences that would aid him in rejecting the bribe, say, by having him hear a menacing voice, in a southern accent of course, say "Do you want to be the husband or the wife?" The key question is whether having this auditory experience would frighten him enough so that he would reject the bribe. If God determines that it will, he exercises a freedom-canceling control over Curley, since it is God, not Curley, who determines Curley's choice. And if God does not determine that it will, he leaves open the possibility that it won't, in which case God's bestowal of grace upon Curley would not realize its intended objective.

Another version of the God-can-do-more objection portrays God as an enabling foreknower. If you hire a person who you know will do a good job and then leave her alone so that she does a good job on her own, you do not cause her not to freely do a good job as you would if you hired her and then caused her to do a good job. You merely create a situation in which she can exercise her free will. Similarly, if God creates a person who he foreknows will always do right, he does not negate her freedom in so acting, as he would if he created her and then rode herd on her to ensure that she always does right. But this solution faces the same problem as did the bestowal-of-grace objection. Can God be assured that if he were to create her, she would always do right. If he determines that this subjunctive conditional proposition is true, he has gone too far and assumed a freedom-canceling controlling over the created person. And if he doesn't determine that it is true, he leaves it open whether it has a favorable truth-value so that his creation of this person ensures that she will always do right. He could be screwed by its contingent truth-value so that he is unable to create her and have her always do right.

Yet another objection is based on God having the power to step in just in the nick of time when he foresees, on the basis of his middle knowledge, that someone will freely go wrong, by either preventing this wrong choice or causally quarantining the culprit from the surrounding world so that no innocent persons are harmed. In the first case, when he foresees on the basis of his middle knowledge that persons will freely go right he leaves them alone, but when he foresees that they won't he cancels their free will just in the nick of time, thereby assuring that all created persons always freely make the right moral choice. The response is that if he adopts this policy of selective intervention, the created persons aren't really free, since to be free with respect to an action is to be free to do it as well as free to refrain from doing it. In the second case, God intervenes after the morally wrong choice is freely made so as to prevent any innocent persons from being harmed. The response to this is that God has bestowed an insignificant sort of free will on his creatures, not the sort of freedom that the theist prizes. It is not enough to have freedom of the will—the freedom to make choices—it also is required that one has freedom of action – the freedom to carry out one's choices and effect one's world for good or ill.

There are two versions of the God-can-do-more variety that are directed against the incompatibilist premise. The first comes from the theological compatibilist who holds that God can determine a free human action, and, moreover, as is the case with Augustine, hold the person morally responsible for the action. The second is that of the soft determinist who contends that a free action can be causally determined, and therefore, God could determine that every created person always freely does right by a proper selection of the scientific laws that obtain and the initial state of the universe, everything that follows, including free actions, being causally determined by the conjunction of these two factors. Both of these compatibilist objections will be responded to in the later discussion.

It is interesting to press an opposite objection to the God-can-do-more variety, namely, that God cannot consistently do as much as is required by Plantinga's FWD. It could be argued that God, in virtue of having middle knowledge, has a freedom-canceling control over created persons. And because these created middlemen aren't free, the buck of moral blame for seeming moral evils cannot stop with them but must reach through to God, which destroys the FWD's attempt to show how God can escape blame, although not responsibility, for these evils. I will begin by marking the distinction between blame and responsibility.

In general, one is responsible for an occurrence that she was fully able to prevent, that is, had the power, opportunity, and necessary knowledge to prevent. God, for example, is responsible for moral evil, since he could have prevented it by electing not to create any free persons. An especially pertinent case is that in which one person delegates some of its power to another but retains the power to revoke the delegated power. In a dual-control student driver car the instructor can throw a switch that gives the student control over the car but still retain the power to regain control over the car by flipping the switch the other way. If the car should be involved in some foreseeable untoward incident while the student is in control, the instructor, along with the student, is responsible, but it could be that only the student is blameworthy. Whether the instructor shares blame will depend on whether she has a good reason for not having retaken control of the car, for example, the resulting harm was minor and the student can best learn by being left free to make mistakes. The relation of God to created free persons is similar. By creating free persons God delegates some of his power to them, but he still retains the power, called "overpower" by Nelson Pike, to rescind their power, either in part or wholly. Because God can withdraw his gift of free will—flip the big switch—he is responsible along with created free persons for the moral evil they cause. But, like the driving instructor, he might have a good excuse that frees him from sharing the blame with those to whom he has delegated some of his power. The FWD supplies such an excuse. God can be responsible but not blameworthy for the evils caused by created beings only if they are free. But, I will now argue, they are not according to the Plantinga

Story of Creation. He never succeeded in flipping the switch that gave them the power to freely control their own lives.

The first stage of the argument establishes that God causes the actions of created free persons according to the FWD in virtue of creating them with knowledge of what will result. Consider this stochastic or indeterministic machine: When its button is pressed, a stochastic or indeterministic process ensues, such as the decay of a radioactive element, the outcome of which determines whether a poisonous gas will be released into a crowded stadium that will result in the deaths of 50,000 innocent people, may result. When the button is pressed, either this outcome will ensue or it won't. Therefore, either it is true that if the button were to be pressed, this horrendous outcome would ensue, or it is true that if the button were pressed, this outcome would not ensue. Let us assume, furthermore, that we mortals cannot discover by any discursive methods which of these subjunctive conditional propositions is true, any more than we can for similarly matched F-conditionals.

Imagine the case in which I chance on the scene and inadvertently press the button, resulting in the horrendous outcome. Given that I did not have "middle knowledge" of what would result from pressing the button and did not intend to bring about or even risk bringing about this outcome, I am blameless for the resulting evils. Furthermore, I do not even cause these evils.

Let us change the circumstances so that I now have "middle knowledge" via some ESP faculty and press the button so as to bring about the deaths. In this case my action is a sufficient cause of the deaths, and is so in spite of the interposition of a stochastic process, which shows that causation can reach through an intervening stochastic process. Furthermore, I am blameworthy for the deaths, unless I have got a mighty good excuse, such as "They were not innocents but terrorists."

Although there is no doubt that this is what people on the street would say, it might be objected that their concept of causation is confused, for the only difference between the two cases is my psychological state, what I know and intend, and how can this determine whether or not I cause the deaths? If what was at issue was the physicist's concept of causation, this would be a powerful objection. But this is not the concept of causation in question. Rather, it is the forensic one that concerns the assignment of moral and legal responsibility and blame, which is the very concept that figures in the FWD, since it is concerned with the assignment of responsibility and blame to God and man for moral evil.

It might be urged by Plantinga that while both God and created free persons were fully able to have prevented moral evil, only the latter are to blame for it, since only God could have a morally exonerating excuse for not doing so. God, not they, is the creator of the universe, and thus he alone could say that his allowing such evil was the price that had to be paid for there existing any free persons at all. The evil in question was necessary for the realization of an outweighing good.

Notice that the response that has been made on Plantinga's behalf does not claim that God does not cause moral evil, only that he is not blameworthy for it since he has an excuse that cannot be available to created free middlemen, and thus they alone take "the fall" for the existence of moral evil. This excuse collapses if these middlemen are not free, since then the buck of blame could not stop with them. And this is just what will now be argued.

Since God creates free persons with middle knowledge of what will ensue, he sufficiently causes the free choices and actions of these persons. This alone does not negate the freedom with which these acts are done, for one person can cause another to act without thereby rendering the act unfree. As a rule, the more the external event only triggers a deep-seated character trait or natural disposition of the agent, the less difficulty there is in treating it as not abrogating the free will of the affected agent. When I induce a person of amorous nature to call Alice for a date by telling him that she is desirous of going out with him, I cause him to act but do not usurp his free will in doing so since prominent among the causes of his action are his own deep-seated character traits, which traits were not imposed on him by me. I didn't have to "work on him" —drug, hypnotize, brainwash, etc. him—to call Alice. Unfortunately, God's way of causing created persons to act is not of this innocent sort. It is freedom-canceling.

The argument for this is anthropomorphic in that it applies the same freedom-canceling principles that apply to man-man cases to the God-man case. Whether it is impermissible, as the theological compatibilist would contend, to reason in this anthropomorphic manner will be considered subsequently. Obviously, any analogy between man and God will be an imperfect one, since there are such striking disanalogies between the two. For this reason this argument hardly is conclusive. At best, it might make a Free Will Defender have second thoughts. I will try to derive these freedom-canceling principles by examining paradigm cases in which one man or finite person has a freedom-canceling control over another.

Imagine the case of The Sinister Cybernetist, a *Stepford Wives*-type situation in which a cyberneticist operates on his wife's brain or replaces it with a pre-programmed computer-analogue so that he can inculcate in his wife the desired psychological makeup comprised of various desires, wants, dispositions, etc. As a consequence, she is always amorous, anxious to cook and clean, etc. To an uninformed observer her actions will appear free and voluntary, since they emanate from and are explainable by her own psychological makeup. But her cyberneticist husband has imposed this makeup on her. Her lack of freedom of the will is not due to the fact that this make-up has been determined by factors external to herself (No man is either an island or a *causa sui*.) but rather to the manner in which it has been determined, namely, through the machinations of another person for the purpose of controlling her responses to stimuli. The case of the Insidious Hypnotist and *Manchurian Candidate*-type Barbaric Brainwasher who have gained an habitual ascendancy over the will of another by inculcating in them a certain psychological makeup are similar.

Our intuitions about these cases suggest the following freedom-canceling sufficient condition for man-man cases:

C_1. If M_1's actions and choices result from psychological conditions that are intentionally determined by another man M_2, then these actions and choices are not free.

Under these circumstances, M_2 has a freedom-canceling control over M_1, not in virtue of determining M_1's actions and choices, but rather causing M_1 not to have a mind or will of her own. It isn't so much M_1's actions and choices that are not free but M_1 herself; and, in virtue of M_1's lack of global freedom, her specific actions and choices are not free. There are good arguments for not taking C_1 alone to be sufficient in every case, but even those who so argue grant that satisfaction of it is at least freedom lessening, which, it will turn out, is enough for my objection.

Consider another case, that of The Evil Puppeteer. Stromboli has poor Pinocchio wired up in such a way that he controls his every movement. An observer who fails to notice the wires might falsely believe that Pinocchio's behavior was fully free and voluntary. Stromboli controls Pinocchio, not via having imposed on him an inner network of dispositions, motivations, intentions, etc., but by exerting a compulsive force over him that renders such inner factors irrelevant.

There need not be actual wires connecting the controller with the "puppet." It could be a wireless radio hookup such as exists between a controller and a remote control toy airplane or between the Horrible Dr. Input and a brain in a vat that in turn has a radio control hookup with a shell body.

By a coincidence that rivals that of the preestablished harmony of Leibniz, it could be the case that every time the external controller causes the "puppet" to perform some movement the "puppet" endeavors on its own to perform this movement. This is a case of causal overdetermination in which there is more than one sufficient cause of a given occurrence. Although the puppet's action is unavoidable in that it would have made this movement even if it had not endeavored to, there are those, like Locke, who would still call it free. Locke's intuition in this matter is quite dubious.

What is it about these cases that makes us say the controller, be it the Evil Puppeteer or the Horrible Dr. Input, has a freedom-canceling control? It is that most of the "victim's" behavior is caused by and subject to the whim of the controller. This suggests that

C_2. M_2 has a freedom-canceling control over M_1 if M_2 causes most of M_1's behavior.

Is God's relation to created persons in the FWD such that it satisfies C_1 and/or C_2? If it satisfies either, no less both, the FWD is in trouble. There is reason to think that it satisfies both. It is clear that it satisfies C_1, since according to the FWD God intentionally causes a created free person to have all of her freedom-neutral properties, which include her psychological makeup. The Free Will Defender will make the Libertarian claim that these inner traits only "incline" but do not causally determine the person to perform various actions or act in a certain regular manner, but this does not make the God-man case significantly disanalogous to the man-man cases. For even if we imagine that our intentional psychological-trait inducers could render it only probable according to various statistical laws that their victims would behave in certain characteristic ways, they still would exercise a global freedom-canceling control in which the person is rendered nonfree due to her not having a mind of her own.

The God-man relation in the FWD also satisfies C_2, for when God instantiates diminished possible persons or sets of freedom-neutral properties he does have middle knowledge of what choices and actions will result, and thereby sufficiently causes them. And he does so quite independently of whether or not he is blameless for the untoward ones among them.

It might be objected that for M_2 to have freedom-canceling control over M_1 it is not enough that M_2 cause most of M_1's behavior: M_2 also must have counterfactual control over M_1 in virtue of which M_2 can cause M_1 to behave in ways other than those in which M_1 in fact behaves. Whereas Stromboli and Dr. Input have this additional counterfactual control over their victims, God does not have it over created persons. For while God causes the instantiator of DP to do A, he does not have the power to cause this instantiator to do other than A, given that it is true that if DP were instantiated, its instantiator would freely do A. God could have prevented the instantiator from doing A by not instantiating DP, but this is not causing the instantiator to do other than A—nonexistent persons do not act.

Granted that there is this disanalogy between God and our finite controllers in that only the latter have this sort of counterfactual control, what follows? Not that God does not have freedom-canceling control over created persons in virtue of satisfying C_2 (as well as C_1), but that there is a stronger sufficient condition for having freedom-canceling control that he does not satisfy, namely,

> C_3. M_2 has a freedom-canceling control over M_1 if M_2 causes most of M_1's behavior and also has the counterfactual power to cause M_1 to act differently from the way in which M_1 in fact acts.

In general, to satisfy one sufficient condition for being X does not require satisfying every sufficient condition for being X. The objector might retort that having counterfactual control is necessary for having freedom-canceling control: The "if" in C_3, accordingly, is to be replaced by "only if." This is not particularly plausible for two reasons. First, if C_3 is turned into a necessary condition, it follows that C_1 is unacceptable and that therefore the Insidious Cyberneticist, etc. do not have freedom-canceling control, which is not what we want to say. Second, God, although lacking counterfactual control, has an additional C_1-type power over created persons that Stromboli and Dr. Input do not have in that he both creates and determines the psychological makeup of his "victims." This additional power of God's, even if it is not freedom-canceling but only freedom-lessening, should at least counterbalance his lack of counterfactual power and thereby make him at least as good a candidate as our finite controllers for having freedom-canceling control.

Furthermore, it should be obvious by now that the FWD's gambit of having something other than God determine the truth-values of the F-conditionals does not succeed in showing that God does not cause the free acts of created persons. Stromboli and Dr. Input were not excused from being the cause of their victim's behavior because they did only "half the job" since they determined the causally relevant instantial conditions but not which causal laws hold. Analogously, God is not excused from being the cause of the free acts of created persons because he did only half the job by determining which diminished possible persons get instantiated but not the truth-values of the relevant F-conditionals. If this does not convince you, try these counterfactual thought-experiments. Our finite controllers do only half the job by determining which causal laws hold after they come upon their victim in some instantial state, and God does only half the job by determining the truth-values of the F-conditionals after he comes upon concrete instantiations of various diminished possible persons. Certainly, we want to say of both God and the finite controllers in these thought-experiments that they cause their "victim's" behavior and have a freedom-canceling control in virtue of C_2 alone.

So far, it appears that God's relation to created persons satisfies both C_1 and C_2 (but not C_3), and that he thereby has a freedom-canceling control over them. But there still remain some disanalogies between the God-man and man-man cases that have not been explored. One of them concerns the fact that the finite controllers in our type 1 and 2 cases were a sinister bunch who meant no good for their victims whereas God is benevolent and intends the best for his created beings. This makes no difference in regard to having freedom-canceling control but only in how the movie is titled. One is titled "The Horrible (Sinister, Insidious, Barbaric) Dr. Input (Cybemeticist, Hypnotist, Brainwasher)" while the other is titled "The Incredible (Fabulous, etc.) Supernatural Predeterminer." One is a horror movie and the other is not; but neither involves free persons.

Another tack is to argue, as would the theological compatibilist, that God's relation to man is so disanalogous to man's relation to man as to render our freedom-canceling principles, C_1 and C_2, that hold for the latter inapplicable to the former. It is not just that God is quite different from men, but that he is different in just those respects that make these principles inapplicable to his relation to created persons.

He literally is out of it, not a part of the universe. No insult intended, but he is as unnatural as you can get; in fact, he is supernatural. He does not cramp our elbow room in the way in which finite men do. Unlike these universe-mates who block our path and physically compel and coerce us, God is not pushing, elbowing, or kneeing anyone in the subway, goosing someone on a crowded elevator or putting a gun to anyone's head ("Your money or your salvation!"). In these respects he is crucially unlike our bevy of sinister finite controllers. These people ride herd on their fellow man. God does not do so. This is not an epistemological point concerning our being unaware of God's causal efficacy in bringing about things in the world, but an ontological one having to do with the radical difference in the way his causal efficacy works from that in which a finite controller's does.

It is just such anti-anthropomorphic considerations that are at the foundation of theological compatibilism. There is much merit in this, but, unfortunately, Plantinga cannot avail himself of this strategy for averting the objection that God assumes a freedom-canceling control over created persons in his FWD. The reason is that his FWD must take the anthropomorphic route in its rejection of theological compatibilism. For it claims that God cannot determine the free acts of persons without negating their freedom. And the only basis for this claim is that if one man were to do this to another it would be freedom-canceling. In other words, God cannot get away with determining the free actions of men, because this would violate C_1 and/or C_2—the very principles that operate in man–man cases.

We cannot allow Plantinga to be a good-time anthropomorphist: To reason anthropomorphically when warding off the objection of the theological compatibilist, and then refuse to do so for the purpose of rebutting the charge that God has assumed a freedom-canceling control over created persons. Thus, Plantinga, is caught on the horns of a dilemma. If he reasons anthropomorphically, his FWD collapses because it imputes to God a freedom-canceling control over created persons. And if he does not reason anthropomorphically, again his FWD collapses, this time because it has no reply to the objection of the theological compatibilist. But either he reasons anthropomorphically or he does not. Therefore, his FWD collapses.

The God-cannot-do-as-much objection has considerable force against the Plantinga version of the FWD, since it imputes middle knowledge to God. Without it, God's instantiating the antecedent of a true F-conditional no longer would count as a case of his causing the instantiator to do what the consequent reports, since he now does not know in advance what this person will do. Created persons, then, could serve as suitable scapegoats for moral evil. This naturally gives rise to the question whether a viable version of a FWD can be constructed that denies middle knowledge to God, that is, that God knows the contingent truth-value of every F-conditional prior to his creative decision and thus foreknows for every diminished possible person what free actions would be performed if that person were it to be instantiated.

It will be recalled that God's middle knowledge is comprised of these two theses:

I. Every F-conditional has a contingent truth-value, that is, is contingently true or contingently false.
II. God knows the truth-value of all F-conditionals, either in the order of time or explanation, prior to his creative decision.

Tenet II is entailed by I because God's omniscience requires him to know every true proposition. Since God's middle knowledge is comprised of the conjunction of theses I and II, there will be two ways of constructing a FWD sans middle knowledge. The first version, which is ably championed by Robert M. Adams, denies I and thereby II, since not even an omniscient being can know what isn't true. This renders God blameless for permitting moral evil, since he could not have known in advance the moral evils that would result from his creation of free persons. The second version accepts I but denies II, again rendering God blameless in virtue of an excusable lack of knowledge. Unlike the first version, there was something to be known but there was no way in which God could have known it. God winds up watching the unfolding of the history of the universe containing free persons in just the way parents watch their child play in a hockey game. In both cases, there are a lot of grimaces and groans as they observe unforeseen errors and transgressions.

Because both versions have God instantiate the antecedent of F-conditionals without foreknowledge of what the created persons will freely do, they face the objection that God is acting in a recklessly immoral way by shooting crap at our expense. No red-blooded theist would accept the wimpy moral intuition underlying the reckless-objection, and would give God's creation of free persons in both versions as a counterexample. The objection also faces an ad hominem-type rebuttal in that no existent person, except for a few gripers, are apt to make it;

for, if God hadn't elected to roll the dice, they wouldn't even exist, and, supposedly, they are glad that they do.

Although both versions make the same lack of knowledge excuse available to God, they differ significantly in their epistemological and metaphysical underpinnings, and thus require separate consideration. Adams develops his version in the course of defending the attack on middle knowledge by certain late sixteenth-century Dominicans against their Jesuit opponents, Molina and Suarez. Adams's denial of I is built upon the Libertarian account of F-conditionals, according to which the act reported by the consequent is not causally determined by prior events, being determined instead by the instantiator's free, causally undetermined choice. Given this account, he does not see how an F-conditional could possibly be true. Thus, it appears to be logically or conceptually impossible for it to be true, and therefore it necessarily lacks a truth-value. Unlike Lukasiewicz's "neuter" or "indeterminate" propositions reporting future contingents, it does not become true or false with the passage of time. Adams says that he doubts if they ever were, or ever will be, true. This means that even if the antecedent should be instantiated and the instantiator subsequently perform the action reported by its consequent, the F-conditional does not become true. And a fortiori this sequence of events does not show that the F-conditional was true all along, for there is no present truth to cast a backward shadow. Adams gives us a choice between F-conditionals being necessarily false and being necessarily neither-true-nor-false. The common denominator of these options is that F-conditionals necessarily are not true.

Adams's argument for the denial of I is not made fully explicit. One who denies I typically is a warranted-assertibility theorist who holds a proposition to be true only if it is in principle epistemically supportable. But this isn't Adams's line, for he says that a proposition reporting a future contingent, although in principle not warrantedly assertible, can be true by *correspondence to* the actual occurrence of the event it predicts. This suggests that for Adams a necessary condition for a proposition being true is that it have an external correspondent. The "external" qualification precludes the correspondent of the proposition that p being the fact that p; for, given that a fact is a true proposition, this would make that p the correspondent of that p.

In the previous discussion of III it was suggested that for Plantinga the external correspondent of the true F-conditional, that if DP were instantiated its instantiator would freely do A, is the abstract diminished possible person *DP* having the funny dispositional property of being-such-that-if-it-were-instantiated-its-instantiator-would-freely-do-*A*. *Pace* Adams, it seems clear that if *DP* were to be instantiated and its instantiator were to do *A*, we would say that *F* was true. Moreover, if *F* were not true, it would not be possible for God to instantiate *P*, as Lewis's lemma states.

It would be a mistake, however, to say that *DP*'s instantiator doing *A* makes *F* true. For this makes it appear as if the instantiator's freely doing *A* is a sufficient *truth-condition* for *F*, being that thing in the world that makes *F* true, in answer to Adams's puzzlement about how an *F*-conditional could be true. But this way of construing the truth-conditions of *F* clashes with the account of its truth-condition based on a diminished possible free person, *DP*, which is an abstract entity, having the funny contingent dispositional property of being-such-that-if-it-were-instantiated-its-instantiator-would-freely-do-*A*. A consequence of this account is that an *F*-conditional can be true even if it is counterfactual because its antecedent goes unactualized; and, even when not counterfactual, it is true prior to the occurrence of the instantiator's action.

The action of the instantiator of *DP* is only a *verifying-condition*, not a *truth-condition*, for *F*. A verifying-condition is what enables us to discover the truth of a proposition but need not coincide with what makes it true. Think in this connection of how you go about indirectly verifying a proposition about the past or about another mind. What makes a proposition about a past event (or another person's conscious state) true is not the future effects of the past event or (the person's overt behavior) by which we indirectly verify it but the past event (or conscious state) itself.

This way of distinguishing between the truth-conditions and verifying-conditions for *F*-conditionals escapes a *reductio ad absurdum* argument against Plantinga's FWD that I owe to Dean Zimmerman. The argument attempts to unearth a vicious circularity in the order of explanation or causation in it. The argument goes as follows. Prior to God's decision to instantiate *DP*, be it in the order of time or that of explanation, God knows that *F* is true. That *F* is true is part of the explanation for his decision to instantiate *DP*, which in turn explains *DP*'s instantiator freely doing *A*, given that it causes his very existence and thus is a necessary cause of *A*. But *DP*'s instantiator freely doing *A* is the truth-condition for *F* and thereby explains why *F* is true, which completes the vicious circle. This vicious circle is broken when *DP*'s instantiator freely doing A is downgraded to a verifying- but not truth-condition for F, since DP's instantiator freely doing A no longer explains why F is true, only how we come to know that F is true. According to this version of the excusable ignorance FWD, what God cannot know prior to his decision to instantiate DP is that the worldly verifying-conditions for F obtain: For, necessarily, before an agent decides, she knows neither what she will decide nor of the occurrence of an event that is dependent on how she decides. Whether the verifying condition for F will occur depends upon whether God chooses to actualize DP.

The other version of the excusable ignorance FWD accepts condition I for middle knowledge, that every F-conditional has a contingent truth-value, as well as Lewis's lemma, but rejects condition II, that God knows the truth-value of all F-conditionals prior to his creative decision. God's morally exonerating excuse for permitting moral evil is that he could not have known in advance what would result from his instantiating various diminished possible person, and, as it sadly worked out, he got screwed by the contingent truth-values of the relevant F-conditionals.

It is plain that in accepting I and rejecting II, the second version rejects the traditional definition of God's omniscience according to which God knows all and believes only true propositions since there are true F-conditionals which he does not know, at least before he chooses to actualize their antecedents. One way to attempt to escape this problem, which Swinburne espoused, is to work with a definition of God's omniscience that is modeled on the definition of his omnipotence. Just as God can bring about anything that it is consistent for him to bring about,

> K. God knows every true proposition that it is logically consistent that God knows.

Since it is an essential property of God that he is able to create free persons and he cannot do so if he knows the truth-values of the F-conditionals in advance of his creative choices, it is inconsistent for God to know their truth-values in advance.

This restriction on God's omniscience was considered in Chapter 1 as a way of excusing the timelessly eternal God from having to know true-tensed propositions, given that it is logically impossible for a being who is not in time to know such a proposition. It was objected to K that it gives God a second-class-type of omniscience, being an especially virulent instance of the paradox of perfection, and, most important, rendered him religiously unavailable to working theists since it precluded his having meaningful personal interaction with them. Whereas it is important that God knows true-tensed propositions, it is important that he *not* know true F-conditionals prior to his creative choices. How can God's omniscience be restricted so that it requires him to know true-tensed propositions but not true F-conditionals? The following is one way of doing this:

K_1. God knows every true proposition that it is logically consistent for him to know and have the ability to create free creatures.

This definition will not appear to be objectionably ad hoc-ish once it is realized that it is an essential property of God that he is able to create free persons but highly dubious that it is an essential property of God that he is timeless and immutable. Notice that the God of my FWD must be temporal, for he changes over time; prior to his creative decision he does not know any F-conditional but after he creates diminished possible free persons he comes to know some F-conditionals in virtue of coming to know their verifying-conditions. By placing God in time and denying him prior knowledge of the F-conditionals we make it possible for God to react to our actions as he is reported to do in the Bible. In a meaningful personal relation there is an element of otherness and mystery. We don't know what the other person will do and therefore have not already made up our minds as to how to act toward the other. There is a processual unfolding of new and unpredictable actions that call for each member in the relation to readjust their behavior toward the other. Given that God essentially is both capable of personal interaction, which requires that he know true-tensed propositions, and capable of creating free persons, which requires that he does not know F-conditionals in advance, definition K will suffice.

EVIDENTIAL ARGUMENTS FROM EVIL

Everyone has been personally touched at some time in their life with a seemingly pointless evil—the premature loss of a loved one, a hideous disease or devastating loss from a natural disaster, and, of course, the horrendous evils that we are bombarded with every time we open a newspaper or turn on the TV. We ask "Why?" but are unable to come up with a satisfying answer. It is the rare person who can say, *and mean it*, "It's God's will and therefore for the best." Most believers find their faith challenged, in many cases lessened or even destroyed. This is a normal human, maybe all too human, reaction. But the question is whether this normal psychological reaction is rationally justified. Are there any good arguments to show that it is? A number of such arguments will be presented and then responded to.

William Rowe has presented an inductive argument that has triggered a flurry of critical responses and counterresponses and thus is a good place to start. His argument is built on two examples of horrendous evils. One is the case of a five-year-old girl, Sue, who is raped, brutally beaten, and then strangled to death, the other a deer, Bambi, who dies a hideously painful death over a period of three days from a forest fire. These cases will be referred to, respectively, by "*S*" and "*B*." Rowe chose to work with these cases because they are the most difficult cases for the theist to find a God-justifying reason for. The argument is based on induction by enumeration and goes like this:

1. No good we know of justifies God, were he to exist, in permitting *S* and *B*.

2. No good justifies God, were he to exist, in permitting *S* and *B*. From 1 by inductive enumeration

3. God does not exist. From 2

The reason why 3 follows from 2 is that 2 reports an unjustified evil, an evil that God, were he to exist, would not have a justification for permitting, and, by definition God and an unjustified evil cannot coexist. Step 2 is inductively derived by simple enumeration from 1 in which we exhaustively consider every good that we know of to see if it could justify God permitting *S* and *B* and find that it cannot. This is similar to examining exhaustively each and every marble in a box and finding that it is not blue and then inferring that no marble in the box is blue.

This exhaustive enumeration goes as follows. Evils *S* and *B*, based on what we know, are completely gratuitous in that they are necessary neither for the realization of an outweighing good nor the prevention of a greater evil. Sue and Bambi are not going to develop higher-order character traits as a result of their struggles against the evils that have befallen them, nor are they going to acquire faith in God because of the realization that pointless evils can randomly happen to anybody.

Certainly, Bambi's demise from the natural disaster cannot be attributed to misuse of free will by herself or anyone else, and, in Sue's case, her attacker exercised his free will but God should not have permitted him to have free will with respect to attacking Sue in the first place; the value of his being free in this regard does not outweigh the harm done to Sue. But not all justified evils are nongratuitous. They could be merited or deserved as punishments for transgressions or be consequences of them and thereby are justified even if they do not serve to reform the wrong doer or deter others from performing similar untoward acts. But certainly Both Sue and Bambi are innocent of any crimes that would call for such harsh punishment.

The search for a God-justifying reason, however, is not as straightforward as looking for a blue marble in a box; for there is a real possibility that we failed either to exhaust all of the justificatory reasons or to see how they might possibly apply in the Sue and Bambi cases. Maybe what is called for is a weaker, probabilistic version of the induction by simple enumeration argument, namely:

1. No good we know of justifies God, were he to exist, in permitting S and B.

2'. It is probable that no good justifies God, were he to exist, in permitting S and B.

3'. It is probable that God does not exist.

There is an even weaker version of the evidential argument that begins with a premise listing all the known cases of evil (call them E).

4. There are evils E.

5. The probability that God exists (G) relative to that there are evils (E) and background knowledge (K) is less than the probability that God exists relative to this background knowledge alone, that is, $P(G/\text{There are evils } E \text{ and } K) < P(G/K)$

The background knowledge K includes everything that we know that is not relevant to determining the truth of either G or that there are evils E. It is not inferred from the proposition that that there are evils E that the probability of G is less than ½, only that that there are evils E lowers the probability of G over what it is relative to K alone. Let us call this version of the probabilistic argument the "modest probabilistic argument" and the preceding one the "strong probabilistic argument."

There is a theistic response to both of these probabilistic arguments that is based on the fact that a proposition's probability can vary relative to different propositions. The probability that Feike can swim relative to the proposition that he is Swiss is quite low, say .1, but relative to the proposition that many people believe that they have seen him swim quite high, near 1, given that seeing is believing. Similarly, the proposition that God exists relative to the conjunction of K and that there are evils E could be quite low but quite high when all of the arguments for the existence of God from Chapter 2 are added to this conjunction. And, if it is probable that God exists relative to the agglomeration of these arguments, then it also is probable that for each evil specified in E there is a God-justifying reason. In fact, if among them is a knock-down ontological argument, we can be certain that there is and thus that there are evils E does not even lower the probability that God exists, as the modest probabilistic argument contends. It was because Leibniz thought he had such an argument that he confined himself in his misnamed book, *The Theodicy*, to sketching some possible *defenses* for God's allowing evil without making any effort to give evidence for their actually obtaining. Saint Augustine did likewise.

As will be seen in Chapter 4, Plantinga believes that we are possessed of a God-implanted *sensus divinitatis* that works in an analogous way to the cognitive faculties of perception and memory in that it too is a source of warranted beliefs that are not based on any evidence or arguments. Because of the *sensus divinitatis* we find ourselves forming the warranted belief that God exists upon reading the Bible, hearing the choir sing, seeing a beautiful sunset, and the like. The probability that God exists relative to the conjunction of this *sensus divinitatis*-derived knowledge and K remains the same when the proposition that there are evils E is added to the conjunction. This completely neutralizes the challenge that E poses for theism IF it is true that God exists and implanted this *sensus divinitatis* in us. But without adequate argumentative support for this, the challenge of evil is still alive and well.

There is another version of the evidential argument from evil in addition to the inductive and probabilistic ones that is based on abduction or inference to the best explanation. It has its roots in Hume's *Dialogues Concerning Natural Religion*. After savaging the teleological argument at length, Hume suddenly has his spokesman in the dialogue, Philo, concede, maybe just for the sake of argument, that there is considerable force to this argument if it is taken to establish only the existence of an intelligent designer-creator of the world, leaving its goodness unresolved. What, he asks, is the most reasonable hypothesis to form concerning its moral nature—that it is all-good, all-bad, morally indifferent, or that there is both a good and bad god, as in Manicheanism. Given that the world is a mixed bag of goods and evils, he claims that the morally indifferent god hypothesis offers the best explanation of the known facts.

Paul Draper has refined Hume's abductive argument. He begins with a proposition, O, that reports the observations one has made of humans and animals experiencing pain or pleasure and the testimony one has encountered concerning the observations others have made of sentient beings experiencing pain or pleasure. Draper then contends that O is better explained by the hypothesis of indifference

> HI. Neither the nature nor the condition of sentient beings on earth is the result of benevolent or malevolent actions performed by nonhuman persons.

than it is by the incompatible theistic hypothesis (T). HI amounts to the anything-but-theism hypothesis, and it is preferable to T because O is more to be expected on HI than it is on T, that is, $P(O/HI){>}P(O/T)$. This expectation is based on the theistic God being omnipotent and omniscient. As will be seen at the end of this chapter, lessening God's power or knowledge provides an easy way for the theist to neutralize the challenge of evil. But at what expense?

William Alston has raised two objections to the Draper argument. First, the argument makes the illicit slide from a proposition being probable relative to another proposition to the latter explaining the former. That a marble that was drawn from a box is green has a very high probability relative to the proposition that almost every marble in the box is green, but the latter hardly explains the former. Furthermore, the adequacy of an explanation depends crucially on the prior probability of the explaining proposition. That I hear rumbling noises in the attic is highly probable on the hypothesis that there are gremlins there; however, because the latter is highly improbable, it does not afford an adequate explanation of the noises. Second, contrasting the hypothesis of indifference explanation of the known pleasures and pains of animals with the theistic one, which says *only* that God caused them, is unfair because it gives too anemic a theistic explanation, omitting the crucial features of it that speak about God's purposes and values, which are the very features that are employed in a theodicy.

THEODICIES

The theist has a battery of responses to all of these evidential arguments, ranging from giving a not implausible God-justifying reason for whatever evil is in question to a skepticism about our being cognitively up to giving such a reason because of the inscrutability of the Divine mind and our limited knowledge of the world. The former is an effort at giving a theodicy, the latter a reason for why no theodicy is needed. First, we will consider efforts to give a theodicy.

It must be stressed at the outset that it is not required that any one theodicy alone do the whole job. What is required is that for every *type* of evil there is some plausible theodicy that applies to it. It might be demanding too much to require that every *instance* of evil be so justified. But unless this latter task is accomplished, the challenge posed by evil to theism is not completely neutralized. Theodicies vary widely with respect to how they conceive of God's goodness and the evidential standards for a theodicy, some requiring only that it not be implausible, others that it is probable relative to the available evidence.

The task of giving a theodicy is greatly lessened if one does not require much of an omnibenevolent being, thus the point of the bumpersticker, "God exists. He just doesn't want to get involved." Richard Swinburne, for example, understands by God's being perfectly good that he does no morally bad action and does any morally obligatory action. Requiring of an omnibenevolent being only that it keep its nose clean, not that it also perform acts of supererogation, plainly sets the bar too low, for many an S.O.B. satisfies this duty-based requirement.

An example of a theodicy that might set this bar too low is Peter van Inwagen's fundamentalist theodicy in which all of the evils reported by *E* are a result of the first generation of humans freely rebelling against God, with their ruin being inherited by all of their descendants. There is no attempt to show that the descendants are in any way blameworthy or morally responsible for these sins, and yet they are the victims of this hereditary ruin. But this seems unfair in just the same way as it is unfair to keep in the whole class for the misdeeds of a single person. The whole idea of a deity who is so vain that if his children do not choose to love and obey him will bring down all sorts of horrible evils on them and their innocent descendants elicits horror from many who would ask what we would think about a human father who treated his children in this way. Like Iago's "Credo" in Verdi's *Otello*, van Inwagen seems to believe in a cruel and vengeful god. His theodicy, by the way, even if successful, does not do the whole job, since it doesn't account for animal suffering, as in the Bambi case unless we include forest fires as another instance of hereditary ruin along with all the other natural evils. Another deficiency in this theodicy is that it is empirically implausible, thereby being at best only a defense.

Consider yet another seeming moral horror to this fundamentalist theodicy by van Inwagen. One of the ways in which God makes it clear that man cannot live apart from him is to create a system of chance evils, the victims of which can be and often are innocent persons, such as Sue. Among the natural consequences of the Fall is the following evil state of affairs: Horrors happen to people without any relation to desert. They happen simply as a matter of chance. It is a part of God's plan of Atonement that we realize that a natural consequence of our living to ourselves is our living in a world that has that feature. Van Inwagen papers over the problem of fairness by the following referential equivocation. *We* complain that some of us— quite often the good and wise and innocent—fall into the pits. God's response to this complaint is this: "*You* are the ones who made yourselves blind," in which the pits represent chance evils and our being blind represents our being defenseless before these evils as a result of hereditary ruin. The use of "we" refers to the innocent descendants of the original culprits who are doing the complaining, but the use of "You" by God refers to the original perpetrators. Herein God is depicted as confounding the perpetrators with their innocent descendants, which is surprising given his omniscience. (I suspect that the equivocation is the fault of van Inwagen rather than God.)

Eleonore Stump has espoused a theodicy that is a close cousin to van Inwagen's in that it too is based on original sin. God brings about natural evils so as to help us achieve salvation, which we do by entering into the proper relationship to him. Our wills have been damaged by original sin and have turned away from God. Natural evils help to realign our wills so that they will again be directed toward serving God by reminding us that we are unable to make it on our own. They humble us by reminding us of how vulnerable and fragile we are, which will aid our coming back to our Lord. They are, however, mere aids; for, if they alone were enough to determine that our wills would become directed toward God, this turning of our wills would not be done freely, which is not what God wants. He wants us to freely elect to return to him. Again, the problem is whether a god who has these moral attributes is eminently worthy of love and worship although not unfit to be eminently worthy of being feared and obeyed—a supernatural Al Capone. This issue will become important in Chapter 4 when we consider pragmatic justifications for having faith.

Axiological problems with theodicies concern not only the type of goodness attributed to God but also the relative values given to wordily goods. Here are some examples of a greater-good theodicy that flagrantly over value certain types of worldly goods. It is good that there is consumption, for if there weren't Verdi never would have written *La Traviata* and Puccini *La Boehme*. Only someone possessed of an Oscar Wilde-type mentality who makes aesthetic values the *summum bonum* would find this plausible. If he hadn't burned down his house in a drunken stupor killing his wife and five children, he never would have given up drinking. Only a member of the Women's Christian Temperance Union would find this at all plausible. My personal favorite example of the if-it-wasn't-for type of theodicy concerns the emergence of good, cheap oriental restaurants in Pittsburgh after the end of the Vietnam War. When I moved to Pittsburgh in 1964 there were only three oriental restaurants in the whole city, all of which served bland Cantonese cuisine. In 1980 I was munching on some delicious sate chicken that I had purchased from a curbside vendor for $3.50 when suddenly it occurred to me that if it weren't for the perverse foreign policy of the United States in Southeast Asia during the 1960s and 70s, I would not have this sate chicken available to me now: It all happened for the best. (The problem with the United States incursions into Afghanistan and Iraq is who wants to eat their food. What must be done is to find a nation with good ethnic food that is underrepresented in the States and then bomb the hell out of them.)

Almost as ludicrous as these parodies of the greater-good theodicy are some of the theodicies that Richard Swinburne devised in his *Providence and Evil*. One example is his attempt to convert the free will *defense* into a free will *theodicy*. To be free with respect to an action having moral significance one must be tempted to choose the morally wrong alternative. Swinburne attributes such great value to persons having this sort of freedom that it justifies God in allowing, for example, Sue's attacker to have the temptation to rape, beat, and strangle her or for persons to be tempted to enslave others. This flies in the face of the moral intuitions that guide our social policies and practices, for we do our best to reform persons who face such temptations and prevent others from having them, thereby preventing them from being free with respect to such actions that can bring great harm to innocent persons. Another example of dubious axiological intuitions is found in Swinburne's deployment of the being-of-service-to-others theodicy to the Bambi case. It is quite possible that Bambi's dying a hideously painful death in the forest fire served as a lesson to other animals as to how to avoid such a fate in the future (or Sue's murder in helping to spur the passage of stronger laws against sexual predators) and this would justify God's permitting this to happen. This looks like more sate chicken for $3.50.

Not all theodicies suffer from dubious axiological assignments either to God or worldly states. Some of them appeal to distinctively Christian values but that alone should not render them nonstarters. An example is the Redemptive Suffering theodicy of Marilyn McCord Adams. It is based upon the value of martyrdom, which then is extrapolatable to some but not all other types of suffering. Through being successfully tested in her faith the martyr builds a closer relation of trust with her God. Furthermore, through suffering one gets a vision into the inner life of God incarnate on the cross. This theodicy has a limited application, doing nothing to address the cases of Sue and Bambi.

The most impressive theodicy is John Hick's free-will-cum-soul-building one. It is based on the reasonable axiological intuition that it is better to achieve some desirable state through one's own free endeavoring than to be in this state from the very beginning or have it imposed on one by some external power. This is a version of a causal theory of value that values a state in terms of how it is brought about. It also is based on an axiological asymmetry between past and future, which is captured by the saying that all's well that ends well as opposed to all's well that begins well. If it is better to be a philosophy professor then a loan shark (a big assumption), then it is better first to be a loan shark and than a philosophy professor rather than vice versa, provided one is the right sort of free, active cause in bringing about this "desirable" development. God could have created human beings in a state of perfection but it is better that he created them in an imperfect state so that they could freely bring about their own moral progress in approximating this ideal state, which, for the Christian, is union or a communal relation with God. God does not merely allow but actually causes natural evils so as to give persons the opportunity to freely develop certain desirable character traits, such as sympathy, charity, courage, patience, and the like. If it be objected that this would license a finite father breaking his sons legs so as to afford him an opportunity for soul-building, the reply is that this confounds the role of God as the designer of the entire scheme of things with that of created persons, which is that of promoting good and fighting evil. Thus, the fact that God is permitted to do things that a human being is not does not result from his being subject to a different moral code than are humans but to the different roles they play.

There are severe limitations in Hick's theodicy, even if its underlying axiological intuitions are accepted. First, it doesn't apply to the vast majority of the known evils, beginning with animal suffering. Often the victim of an evil is so devastated that she is unable to put it to the positive use of aiding her moral development, as for example Sue or the child who succumbs to leukemia at the age of one. That the parents of Sue or the leukemia victim are afforded an opportunity for soul-building hardly suffices to justify the evils in question. To handle these recalcitrant cases Hick has supplemented his theodicy with a compensation-in-an-afterlife one. But the latter is nothing more than a defense, since the evidential credentials for it are very thin.

In addition to the limited range of application of Hick's theodicy, there is a problem about the cases to which it does apply in that they seem to involve more evil than is required for the sake of spurring soul-building. One can develop sympathy and charity in response to a single person's suffering from hunger or disease; it doesn't require one million. The response is that the objector commits the slippery-slope fallacy when she charges that any evil, however slight, is not justified since it is possible for God to further his soul-building project with an even smaller evil. An objection that can be raised no matter what the circumstances are is not a legitimate objection. The God–could–have–done-better objection has been raised against the widely offered significant-contrast theodicy that justifies God's allowing evil because we could not appreciate the good without a contrast with evil. Supposedly he could have achieved this objective without allowing as much evil as he did. Again, it is an objection that can be raised no matter how small the quantity of allowed evil is. There is a more telling objection to this theodicy that contends that God could have created us with a different psychological makeup that would have enabled us to appreciate the good without having in our experience any significant contrast with evil.

There is a very fanciful theistic response to the God-could-do-more objection that I owe to Donald Turner. Traditional theism assumed that God elected to actualize one and only one of the infinitely many possible worlds. But a case can be made out that God's omnibenevolence requires him to create as much good as possible—let the good times roll, the more the merrier—which would result in his actualizing every possible world in which there is a favorable balance of good over evil. It should not surprise us, therefore, that the world we inhabit contains some evil. All that we should expect, if we are theists, is that it is overall a world worth having, because it contains a favorable balance of good over evil. There aren't many takers for this many-world theodicy, no doubt because it deflates our ego, just as did the Copernican discovery that we are not geographically the center of the universe or the news that a baby brother has just been born so that our parents will love us less. Are these good reasons?

There is yet another way of blocking this God-could-do-more objection. If God were to have created us with a different psychology than we in fact have, the causal laws of science would have had to be different, but van Inwagen has questioned whether this is possible. He refers to some respected physicists who claim that the causal laws that hold for the actual world are the only possible ones. He defends a doctrine of modal skepticism about possibility and necessity claims that transcend our ordinary, everyday experiences. It is okay to have such modal intuitions. He himself has them, since as a committed theist he believes that it is possible for there to be a creation *ex nihilo*. What we are not permitted to do is to employ one of these dubious modal intuitions as a premise in an argument; for then the onus falls on us to justify it, and this cannot be done. For example, we cannot justify the claim that God could have created water that would not drown, fire that would not burn, and wild tigers that would not be carnivores, or at least some reasonable facsimiles of them, since to do so we would have to be able to design the causal structure of a universe in which these things obtain. And this we cannot do.

Van Inwagen fails to notice that many theodicies, including some that he gives, violate his modal skepticism, since they employ a dubious modal premise or a premise that entails a dubious modal proposition, such as that it is possible that original sin caused hereditary ruin and that it is possible that humans will survive death in a Christian type of heaven. Furthermore, the manner in which van Inwagen defends and deploys his modal skepticism is quite dubious. It seems obvious to most physicists that a different law of gravity could have obtained, for example, one that has a different value for the gravitational constant. They would view his opposing modal intuition as qualifying him for nonvoluntary commitment to the EMIDS (Extreme Modal Intuition Deficiency Syndrome) Foundation hospital. Van Inwagen, of course, has rooms in his own EMIDS hospital that await the involuntary commitment of his rivals. It is interesting to note that if the causal structure of the universe is necessary, van Inwagen's God winds up as limited God that is in the same fix as the Demiurge in Plato's *Timaeus* who is limited by the principle of necessity inherent in the stuff—the Receptacle—that he is given to work with. This solves the problem of evil. But it remains to be determined at what price.

THEISTIC SKEPTICISM

So far only theodical responses to the evidential arguments from evil have been considered. But by far the most favored response among sophisticated contemporary theorists, most notably Alston, Plantinga, Wykstra, and van Inwagen, is that of theistic skepticism. Because our imaginative and cognitive powers are so radically limited, we are not warranted in inferring that there are not or probably are not God-justifying reasons for evils *E*. Theistic skepticism involves our inability, first, to access the divine mind so as to determine the different sorts of reasons that God could have for permitting evil and, second, to determine whether some purported God-justifying reason applies to a given case of evil. The former will be called "reason skepticism" and the latter "application skepticism." Defenders of theistic skepticism invariably supplement it with some speculation about possible defenses or theodicies for *E*. This is fitting, since the believer must have some target for her faith, however sketchy and evidentially unsupported it is.

Rowe's argument based on exhaustive enumeration mistakenly assumes that we are up to divining every possible God-justifying reason for permitting evil. As Stephen Wykstra has put it, God's reasons are no-see-ums for us. If you carefully inspect a room and fail to detect a zebra, it is reasonable for you to inductively infer that there is no zebra in the room. But if you were trying to detect an ammonia molecule in the room, your failure to find it by unaided observation would not justify your inference that no ammonia molecule is in the room. The Divine mind is the ultimate no-see-um for us, regardless of what instruments of detection we employ. Our minds are to God's as a one-month-old baby's is to an adult's mind. It is contended that a universe created by God would likely have great moral depth in that many of the goods below its puzzling observable surface, many of the moral causes of God's current allowings and intervenings, would be "deep" moral goods. Alston develops an analogy between the physical world and morality in respect to their having a hidden nature that is gradually brought to light by painstaking investigation.

This analogy appears strained. To discover the hidden nature of gold, its molecular structure, required a long-term, sustained inquiry. But no analogous inquiry was required to unearth the hidden nature of morality, for a hidden morality is no morality. The "discovery" that love is better than hate because it is more affectionate is quite different from the discovery that gold has a certain atomic weight and number. To be sure, some of our primitive progenitors in the evolutionary process did not recognize any moral rules and principles, but that no more shows that we had to perform inquiries over a long period of time analogous to those employed by scientists to discover the inner nature of morality than does the fact that they blew their noses on the ground while we use Kleenex shows that we had to inquire deeply into the nature of nose blowing. No doubt we have a heightened moral sensitivity relative to them, but that is not due to our having unearthed the deep, hidden nature of morality.

That morality be on the surface, common knowledge of all, is an empirical presupposition for our engaging in our social moral practices, the purpose of which is to enable us to modify and control each other's conduct by the use of generally accepted rules and principles of moral evaluation, thereby effecting more satisfactory social interactions. It also is required for our entering into relationships of love and friendship with each other. Such relationships require significant commonality of purposes, values, sympathies, ways of thinking and acting, and the like.

Many objections have been lodged against theistic skepticism. One is that it precludes the theist from employing teleological arguments, although not ontological and cosmological arguments; for, if the bad things about the world should not be evidence against the existence of God, the good things should not count in favor of his existence. Teleological arguments turn into two-edged swords. Maybe the good aspects of the world that these arguments appeal to are produced by a malevolent deity so as to highlight evil or because they are necessary for the realization of an outweighing evil, and so on for all the other demonodicies.

The most serious problem for theistic skepticism, which is raised by Bruce Russell, is that it seems to require that we become complete moral skeptics. Should we be horrified at what happened to Sue? Should we have tried to prevent it or take steps to prevent similar incidents in the future? Who knows? For all we can tell it might be a blessing in disguise or serve some God–justifying reason that is too "deep" for us to access: For example, it might be a merited Divine punishment for some misdeed that Sue will commit in the after-life. The result of this moral skepticism is paralysis of the will, since we can have no reason for acting, given that we are completely in the dark whether the consequences of our action is good or bad.

Another objection concerns whether theistic skepticism allows for there to be a meaningful personal love relation with God. The problem concerns whether we humans can have such a relation with a being whose mind so completely transcends ours, who is so inscrutable with respect to his values, reasons, and intentions. Not all kinds of moral inscrutability preclude a love relationship. It is important to distinguish between the moral rules and principles employed by a person and the manner in which she applies them to specific cases based on her knowledge of the relevant circumstances, this being a casuistic issue. A distinction can be made between moral principle inscrutability and casuistic inscrutability. That another person is casuistically inscrutable to us need not prevent our entering into a communal love relationship with it, provided it is far more knowl-edgeable than us about relevant worldly conditions, as is God, an omniscient being. But moral principle inscrutability of a certain sort does rule out such a relationship. Although we need not understand all of the beloved's moral reasons for her behavior, it must be the case that, *for the most part*, we do in respect to behavior which vitally affects ourselves. One thing, and maybe the only thing, that can be said in favor of the theodicy favored by fundamentalists according to which all the evils reported by E result from the Fall and are messages from God to show us how lost we are without him, is that it does not run afoul of this requirement. We can hardly love someone who intentionally hurts us and keeps his reasons a secret unless for the most part we know his reasons for affecting us as he does and moreover know that they are benevolent. The answer to Plantinga's rhetorical question that if God did have a reason for permitting evil, why should we be the first to know, is that we should be for those that vitally concern us, at least for the most part. No doubt, the theistic skeptic will respond that this is being too anthropomorphic in its likening of a man-God personal relation to a man–man personal relation. This is a continuation of our discussion in Chapter 1 as to how anthropomorphic our concept of God, which was at the heart of the choice between a God that is timelessly eternal rather than omnitemporally eternal.

Making God so inscrutable also raises a threat that theism thereby will turn out to be falsified or, if not falsified, rendered meaningless. Several atheists, including Michael Scriven and Theodore Drange, have used the hiddenness of God as the basis for an argument against his existence. There is, they say, a presumption of atheism so that no news is bad news. Numerous quotations from the Bible are assembled in which it is said that God's intention in creating men was so that they would come to know of his existence and worship, obey, and enter into a communal loving relation with him. Thus, if we do not have good evidence that God exists because he has chosen to remain hidden, this constitutes good evidence against his existence.

Swinburne has an answer to this atheistic argument that is based on God wanting created persons to come to know of his existence and enter into a communal relation with him of their own free will. If he were to make his existence too obvious, this would necessitate their doing so and thus be freedom-canceling. If God's existence, justice, and intentions became items of evident common knowledge, then man's freedom would in effect be vastly curtailed. An ontological argument would do even greater violence to the traditional Christian view of God as wanting men to come to know, love, and obey him of their own free will. If someone were to come up with a really convincing version of the ontological argument, Swinburne might not be crushed if we followed the example of the Pythagoreans, who set adrift sans supplies the person who demonstrated the existence of irrational numbers. Again, we see Swinburne radically over-estimating the value of free will. A consequence of his position is that we should not raise our children in a religion, since then their subsequent religious belief will not have been acquired freely. Swinburne has mislocated the point at which free will enters into the religious life. It is not in regard to one's believing that God exists but how she lives up to this belief in her life.

By not allowing known evils E to count against God's existence, not even allowing them to lower the probability that he exists, the skeptical theist might be draining the theistic hypothesis of all meaning. E is itself a staggering array of evils, many of the most horrendous sort. If E is not the least bit probability lowering, then it would appear that for theistic skeptics no amount of evil would be. Even if the world were a living hell in which each sentient being's life was one of unrelenting suffering of the worst sort, it would not count as evidence against God's existence, would not lower the probability of his existence one bit. This seems highly implausible and calls into question the very meaningfulness of their claim that God exists. And this is so whether or not we accept the notorious verifiability theory of meaningfulness, which Plantinga likes to have die the death of self-reference by pointedly asking whether it is applicable to itself. We can recognize that something has gone wrong even if we cannot come up with a good theoretical explanation of why it is wrong.

That E is not probability lowering will come as news to the working theist who sees the evils reported by E as counterevidence to God's existence that tries her faith. The response of defensive skeptics, such as Plantinga, is to make a distinction between the pastoral and epistemic problem of evil. What this amounts to, though they wouldn't want to put it this bluntly, is that the working theist whose faith is strained or endangered by the evils which directly confront her is emotionally overwrought and not able to take the cool stance of the epistemologist of religion and thereby see that these evils, however extensive and seemingly gratuitous, are really no challenge to her theistic beliefs. Since she is unable to philosophize clearly at her time of emotional upset, she needs the pastor to hold her hand and say whatever might help her to make it through the night and retain her faith in God.

There is a problem here; however, it is not a pastoral problem but a problem with the pastor and the theistic skeptic who runs such a line. Her crisis of faith, although rationally explainable in terms of psychological causes, is not rationally justified because it rests upon the epistemically unwarranted belief that the evils confronting her probably are gratuitous or, at least, counterevidence to God's existence. It also follows that her emotion of horror at the evil of the holocaust, for example, is equally irrational because based on the epistemically unwarranted belief that the apparent gratuitousness of this evil lessens the likelihood that God exists. Rationally speaking, she ought not to feel horror at the holocaust!

Theistic skepticism appears to be an ivory tower invention of the detached epistemologist of religion that is completely out of touch with the grimy realities of everyday religious faith and experience. By neutralizing the dramatic bite of evil, it makes it too easy to have religious faith, as Kierkegaard might say. There are responses to all of the objections that have been raised against theistic skepticism, but because of space limitations we will exit the tennis match here, bearing in mind that the rally has not come to an end, nor will it ever.

We have yet to consider one rather obvious way for theists to meet the challenge of evil—go with a finite God, as do process theologians like Alfred North Whitehead and Charles Hartshorne. There are many ways to achieve this, since God has many omniperfections that can be tinkered with. No theist wants to downgrade his omnibenevolence, since this would preclude God from playing the role of an eminently worshipable being. It has already been seen in this chapter how tinkering with his omniscience can create a defense of God for permitting moral evil.

Here is a fanciful, never before given way of playing with his omniscience that would give him an excuse for allowing evils E. God's omniscience does not extend to knowing metaphysical truths. Assume that Bishop Berkeley's metaphysical theory of matter is right. Material objects are nothing but coherent congeries of ideas in different minds, including God's. Berkeley's gloss on the account of Divine creation in *Genesis* is that God creates the heavens and earth by coherently ideating in a heavenly and earthlike manner. Imagine that God is in the process of deliberating about what world to create and innocently imagines a quite defective world, namely ours, without having any intention to create it. Being unaware of metaphysical truths, he fails to realize that he is thereby creating this world. Upon learning that, he said, "Oops, sorry about that."

This story at least holds on to his omnibenevolence. The only thing wrong with it is Berkeley's idealist theory of matter. The most obvious omniperfection to downgrade is omnipotence, which brings us back to the Demiurge of Plato's *Timaeus*. Like a sculptor who is given a block of marble to work with that limits what he can create because it has a nature of its own, this god is given stuff to work with that limits what he can create. But if God is not all-powerful, how powerful is he? Does not this account of God's excuse for allowing evil run into the same unfalsifiability-in-principle problem as did theistic skepticism? No matter how much evil there is, the response is that he is just not *that* powerful, which resembles the punch-line of the famous shaggy dog joke, "Yes, he was a shaggy dog, but he wasn't *that* shaggy."

4

Nonevidential
Justifications of Belief

S o far we have considered attempts to show that theism is evidentially or epistemically justified and the contrary attempts to show
that agnosticism or atheism is, the former resting on the battery of
theistic arguments in Chapter 2 and the latter on arguments from evil
and the hiddenness of God in Chapter 3. But maybe it was a mistake
to seek epistemic justification for theism. Maybe it does not need any
justification. Or maybe some kind of nonepistemic justification can
be given for or against it. Both of these possibilities will be explored
in this chapter.

NONCOGNITIVISM

One way of establishing that religious utterances do not require any
epistemic justification is to take them as not making any truth-claims.
Since they are not used to refer to God and make true or false claims
about him, there is nothing to be epistemically justified. This decog-
nifying of them has the apologetic upshot of making them impervious
to challenges from science regarding the world's past, its composition,
and the naturalistic causes of religious belief and experience. There is
a *descriptive* version of noncognitivism that purports to describe how
"God"-talk is employed in our actual practice of religion and a

revisionary version that makes no such pretension but instead pre-scribes that we decognify our use of religious language.

An explicitly revisionary version is given by Richard Braithwaite, who wants to reconstruct our religious practices so that they become a communal device for instilling ethical attitudes in people through the telling of emotionally charged Biblical stories and parables, under-stood now as mere myths. The religion of Ethical Culture is an example of the reduction of religion to ethical practice. John Dewey, in his *A Common Faith*, advocated something similar—that institutio-nalized religion provide people with an opportunity to give public expression to their ideal ends that serve to unify each person's life as well as unify each person to every other one in a democratic society. Faith would no longer be faith in a supernatural God but faith in human intelligence, aided by friendly forces within nature, to ame-liorate the problems of men. It is doubtful whether people who practice "good old-time religion" would find this pale humanistic substitute adequate. The motivation behind these revisionary accounts of religion is moral, namely that we shall do better with these humanistic religions than we have done with the traditional ones. This issue falls outside the purview of this book, which is concerned with how good old-time religious belief can be justified.

The descriptive version, if it succeeds in describing anything, describes the use of religious language by a very tiny, sophisticated minority such as might be found in the philosophy departments at Oxford and Cambridge. It is defended in *The Unknown God* by a Wittgenstein disciple, Antony Kenny, who claimed that it is quite impossible to speak about God, for he is not something to be captured by human language. We cannot speak of God literally. But if "God"-talk has no literal meaning, what sort of meaning does it have? Although God is completely ineffable, we can speak of God *poetically* and *metaphorically*. His likening of religious discourse to poetry is no help, since poetry is a style of writing and does not address the content, or lack thereof, of what is expressed and, in particular, whether it should be interpreted literally. One can poetically make factual claims. That we should understand religious language meta-phorically also is unhelpful, for a metaphor has some literal content. To say that Jones is a lion, although it does not mean that he is literally a lion, does entail that he literally has some of the distinctive traits of lions, most notably, courage. Furthermore, I must be able to refer to Jones, and this can be accomplished only by an explicit or implicit covering sortal term, such as manhood. Thus, Kenny contradicts himself when he says that God can be spoken about metaphorically although he is ineffable. Kenny's nonliteralism comes to the same thing as atheism.

Another way that Kenny inconsistently tries to explain his ineffability thesis is by an endorsement of Wittgenstein's position on the mystical in his *Tractatus* according to which the mystical *shows* itself even though we cannot *say* anything about it, which is the basis of his famous remark that whereof one cannot speak, thereof one must be silent. Unfortunately, Wittgenstein not only failed to demarcate what can be said from what can only be shown, but also contradicted himself when he said that the mystical shows itself although nothing can be said about it.

In the first place, in the ordinary sense of say and show there is no dichotomy between them, since what can be shown also can be said or described. For example, I can both show you some lace off Queen Anne's wedding dress and also describe it. Since 'say' and 'show' are being used in an eccentric sense, some explanation of their meaning is required. But neither Wittgenstein nor his legions of disciples have come anywhere close to supplying this needed explanation. Furthermore, Wittgenstein's claim that the mystical shows itself although it cannot be spoken about is inconsistent, for we would not be able to determine that it was experientially given unless we possessed some understanding of what the mystical is. Mystics, in spite of their protestations of ineffability, manage quite well to describe their experiences, even for the straight community of nonmystics, at least to the extent that nonmystics would know if they some day were to have an experience meeting this description. Of course, mystical descriptions cannot fully capture what they describe, but this is true of language in general, since there is not a qualitative isomorphism between symbols and what is symbolized. The word "passion" does not have its breath coming in short pants.

The most disturbing part of Wittgenstein's saying-showing dichotomy is his complete failure to give an adequate criterion for what can be said. What can be said, according to him, is what can be expressed by atomic propositions and truth-functions thereof, in which a truth-value proposition is one whose truth-value is uniquely determined by the truth-values of its constituent propositions. The problem is not that Wittgenstein was unable to produce any examples of an atomic proposition but that the very concept of an atomic proposition is an impossible one. On the one hand, an atomic proposition is claimed to be informative, in fact, the only thing that is, but, on the other hand, no atomic proposition entails any other atomic proposition or its negation. For this reason "*a* is red" and "*a* is two feet from *b*" fail to be atomic, since the former entails "*a* is not blue" and the latter that "*a* is not three feet from *b*." Obviously, if "*a* is red" is atomic so is "*a* is blue" and thus neither is an atomic proposition. The same holds for sentences that contain predicates expressing values for the physical parameters of different scientific theories. But to be informative, a sentence must have a predicate that excludes other things; the more it excludes, the more informative it is. But the predicate of an atomic proposition, whether monadic or relational, excludes nothing.

LANGUAGE-GAME FIDEISM

Wittgenstein said a lot of things about religion, not all of which spoke for nonliteralism. Several of his followers, among whom are Norman Malcolm, D. Z. Phillips, and R. M. Hare, found a doctrine of "language-game fideism" in his writings. A language-game is a normative rule-governed linguistic practice. The rules need not be explicitly formulated, but they enter into the playing of the game because the participants are willing to offer corrections and accept corrections when there is a deviation from them. In *On Certainty*, Wittgenstein claimed that for each language-game there are framework-constituting principles that one must accept if they are to engage in it. For the language-games of making material object claims on the basis of sense experience, claims about the past on the basis of apparent memories, and claims about the future on the basis of inductive reasoning, they are, respectively, that in general our senses, apparent memories, and inductive reasoning are reliable. Attempts to justify these framework-constituting principles invariably fall prey to vicious epistemic circularity in that some premise must be employed that can be known only by appeal to what is vouchsafed by the use of the faculty in question. As Hume so clearly brought out, attempts to justify induction make use of inductive reasoning when they say that inductive reasoning will continue to work in the future because it has worked in the past. Our beliefs in these framework-constituting principles, therefore, are groundless. If asked to justify one of these language-games, the best that one can do is to say that this is what we do, this is who we are, this is our form of life.

There is a religious language-game that is analogous to these language-games. Like them, it has its own framework-constituting principles and internal criteria for a belief being rationally warranted. Furthermore, like the sense and memory language-games it has its own ontology. Whereas they presuppose, respectively, the existence of material objects and past events, the religious language-game presupposes the existence of God. And it further resembles these games in having its own internal criteria of what constitutes a rationally warranted belief about the individuals in its ontology, such as that it is warranted to believe that God exists on the basis of apparent direct nonsensory perceptions of him or experiences that one has upon reading the Bible. It would be just as inappropriate for a participant in the religious language-game to ask whether God really exist or whether some evil is unjustified as it would be for a participant in the sense experience language-game to ask whether material objects really exist or someone engaged in the fiction storytelling language-game to ask whether the beautiful princess really existed?"

By making warrant, rationality, and ontology internal to a language-game, language-game fideism achieves the same apologetic goal as does nonliteralism in that it makes the religious language-game invulnerable to hostile external challenges, but without paying the price of giving a distorted depiction of the actual practice of religion, as does nonliteralism. If asked to justify religious belief and practice, the answer is the greatest story ever told, "The language-game is played." End of story! In protecting their cherished language-game, some language-game fideists go so far as to claim that only someone who is an active participant in it can even understand the game. One wonders how it is possible to convert to a religion since one would not know what he is converting to.

It is doubtful, however, as Michael Martin forcefully argued, that language-games exist in such splendid isolation from each other so that the belief-outputs of one cannot be used to challenge those of another. Here is where the analogy between ordinary games and language falters. Games are isolated activities that one chooses to play—"Tennis anyone?" But the religious language-game makes use of the same principles of reasoning as are employed in the scientific and ordinary sense experience language-games. It also refers to the same world that they do, thus the absurdity of Wittgenstein's claim that if someone believes that there will be a day of final judgment and another does not, they do not disagree. It seems plain that the religious and nonreligious persons are making incompatible claims with regard to the very same future. Likewise, the account of creation in *Genesis* is making claims upon the very same past that modern cosmology does, only incompatible ones. This provides an external standpoint from which to criticize the religious language-game. It was seen in Chapter 3 how evil can be a basis for an external challenge to theism. Appeal to our ordinary moral intuitions can also serve as an external ground for criticizing certain religious language-games that are sexist, imperialistic, and racist. There really is only one big language-game of which all the many different language-games are interrelated parts. If the religious language-game were as isolated and self-contained as language-game fideists maintain, it would die the death of triviality since it would have no relevance for our life in the workaday world.

BASICALLY WARRANTED THEISTIC BELIEF

Alvin Plantinga has made a valiant attempt to show that it is possible for theistic belief to be nonevidentially epistemically warranted. From his initial book on *God and Other Minds* in 1967 to his monumental *Warrant and Christian Belief* in 2000, he has defended theism by lodging a circumstantial *ad hominem* objection against his nontheist opponents in which it is argued that they uphold epistemic standards for theistic belief that their own nontheistic beliefs fail to satisfy. It has just been seen how language-game fideists make this charge against their atheistic opponents. It is widely assumed, as part of our Lockean legacy, that a belief that God exists can be epistemically rational, justified, or warranted only if it has adequate evidential support from beliefs that are either self-evident or evident to our senses. Without suitable argumentative support, theistic belief fails to measure up to proper epistemic standards and thereby violates our epistemic duties. Alvin Plantinga, who accepted this evidentialist assumption in his writings prior to the early 1980s, mounts a vigorous attack on it in *Warranted Christian Belief*. He had argued with considerable force in *Warrant: the Current Debate* and *Warrant and Proper Function* that what warrants a "basic belief," a belief that is not based on or inferred from another belief, is that it results from the proper functioning of one's cognitive faculties in the right kind of epistemic environment according to a design plan successfully aimed at truth.

Plantinga begins with basic beliefs that arise from our senses, memory, introspection, sympathy, and *a priori* reason, which comprise the "standard package" of cognitive faculties. He makes out a powerful case in these two earlier *Warrant* books that such beliefs are warranted when the faculty that produces them is functioning properly in the right sort of epistemic environment according to a design plan aimed at seeking truth. Someone who seems to see a tomato and then believes that there is a tomato out there has a warranted belief and moreover knows that there is a tomato out there. His warrant for believing this, however, is subject to defeaters or overriders concerning something that is abnormal about his faculty of vision (he has cataracts) or the epistemic circumstances (he is in a factory that manufactures plastic tomatoes). Let us, for the sake of argument, accept this account of warrant.

The next step in Plantinga's argument is to show that it is possible that theistic, and in particular Christian, beliefs have warrant in an analogous way to that in which sensory and memory beliefs, etc., do. If theism is true, then God would want to reveal himself to created persons. Toward this end he implanted in them as part of their original cognitive equipment, along with the cognitive faculties in the standard package, a *sensus divinitatis* that would enable them to form true non-inferential beliefs about God's presence, nature, and intentions upon having certain experiences, such as reading the Scriptures, hearing the choir sing, seeing a beautiful sunset, feeling guilt, and so on. Provided their *sensus divinitatis* is functioning properly on these occasions in accordance with its divinely determined design plan in the right sort of epistemic environment, their basic beliefs are warranted and constitute knowledge even if the subjects of the experiences are unable to offer any argument or justification for their beliefs. That they have such a noninferential warrant does not preclude them also to have an evidentialist-based warrant: Plantinga is no fideist.

Plantinga also introduces a special supernatural process involving the internal instigation of the Holy Spirit by which one is directly caused by God, without any intervening worldly causes, to believe the great things of the Gospel concerning the incarnation, resurrection, salvation, and the like. Plantinga does not argue that these people are in fact warranted in their basic beliefs, only that it is possible that they are. To do the former would require giving evidence or arguments that God exists and has set things up the way in which Plantinga's so-called Aquinas/Calvin model (A/C for short) says that he has.

The analogy between the *sensus divinitatis* and the cognitive faculties of the standard package runs throughout *Warranted Christian Belief* and is central to the case that Plantinga constructs for it being possible to have a warranted basic belief in God. The heart of the analogy is that we can predicate of both types of experience the notion of being produced by a cognitive faculty that is "functioning properly," as contrasted with one that suffers from a "disease," "dysfunction," "malfunction," "pathology," or "disorder," to use Plantinga's terminology. A dilemma argument can be constructed in regard to the predication of these terms. Either they are supposed to be predicated in the same sense of both theistic and standard package beliefs or they are not. On both alternatives Plantinga's argument for the possibility of theistic and, in particular, Christian belief being warranted fares badly.

If Plantinga assumes that they are predicated in the same sense, he winds up with a false analogy. For there are agreed–upon objective tests for a cognitive faculty in the standard package being in a state of dysfunction, malfunction, pathology, or disorder. But it is obvious that there are no agreed–upon objective tests for a person's *sensus divinitatis* suffering from a dysfunction, malfunction, pathology, or disorder. It will not do to charge this objection with resting on an unacceptable verificationist principle, for the point of the objection is not that every type of cognitive experience must admit of a distinction between proper and improper functioning that measures up to verificationist standards, only that Plantinga's analogically-based argument commits him to this being so for his *sensus divinitatis* since it is true of the cognitive faculties in the standard package.

In regard to basic religious beliefs that are internally instigated by the Holy Spirit, it is obvious that the notion of proper functioning could have no application to them since they are supernaturally caused directly by God. Such instigation, furthermore, is not a faculty but a process and thus cannot be said to have any function and therefore cannot be said to malfunction or be subject to a pathology; for there is no correct way for God to supernaturally cause worldly occurrences.

Plantinga continually talks about the *sensus divinitatis* in natural law terms; but, whereas for Aristotelian natural law theorists questions concerning an individual's nature and proper mode of functioning are to be answered, at least in part, by empirical inquiry, there is nothing analogous in regard to determining the nature and proper functioning of the *sensus divinitatis* or for what constitutes a proper way for the internal instigation of the Holy Spirit to occur.

There are further damaging disanalogies between Plantinga's A/C experiences and those in the standard package. Whereas there is universal participation in the very same doxastic practices based on the experiences in the standard package, this is not so for *sensus divinitatis*-based experiences. Plantinga has an explanation for this disanalogy based upon the serious damage that the *sensus divinitatis* suffered as a result of Original Sin, a damage that is reparable only by the supernatural intervention of the Holy Spirit. But to explain why there is this disanalogy does not explain it away.

Another disanalogy is that there is no standard package analogue to religious diversity. There is widespread disagreement among persons of different religions in regard to how they respond to reading the *New Testament* in that only some find themselves suddenly believing that a triune God exists whose Son has atoned for our sins. In contrast, persons have pretty much the same doxastic responses to their standard package experiences.

The multivocalist horn of the dilemma fares no better than does the univocalist one. Plantinga now is to say that these terms are predicated with a different sense of the two kinds of basic beliefs. Herein Plantinga cannot make use of the results established by his two earlier *Warrant* books in his argument for the possibility of having a warranted basic belief that God exists. Thus, his basic A/C experiences can be said to admit of the dysfunction–proper function distinction just as do standard package beliefs, only the tests for the former will be radically different from those for the latter. Whereas the latter are based on empirical tests that have a grounding in what is vouchsafed by science, the latter will be based on criteria that are internal to the different religious doxastic practices and thus will vary across these practices, thereby posing the problem of religious diversity. And this is language-game fideism, a doctrine that has just been found to be highly problematic and one that Plantinga's ardent theological realism rejects.

Plantinga has made the bold claim that if theism is true, then something like his account of warranted basic theistic belief is true. And, on the basis of this conditional proposition, he infers, by the law of *modus tollens*, that a denial that basic theistic belief is warranted in pretty much the same way as his model depicts, also denies the truth of theism. The *de facto* issue of the truth of theism, therefore, cannot be separated, as many have claimed, from the *de jure* issue of the warrant for theistic belief. If the objections to Plantinga's model are justified, then the *modus tollens* refutation of theism fails, since the conditional proposition in question is false. If theistic and, more specifically, Christian beliefs are to be warranted, they must be warranted in some manner that is radically disanalogous to the way in which standard package beliefs are. This robs Plantinga of his circumstantial *ad hominem* response to his atheistic opponents for setting a higher epistemic standard for theistic belief than they do for beliefs based on the faculties in the standard package.

Another problem with Plantinga's A/C model of basic warrant of theistic belief is that it might not escape the need to appeal to evidence, merely relocating the place at which appeal must be made to it. Philip Quinn has argued that for intellectually sophisticated adults in our culture there are defeaters for Plantinga-type basic beliefs in God consisting in the prevalence of apparently unjustified evils and certain naturalistic explanations for religious beliefs. While Plantinga reject's Quinn's claim that there are defeaters for his basic beliefs in God, he agrees with him to this extent: There are at least potential defeaters that Quinn's "intellectually sophisticated adults in our culture" must neutralize if their basic belief in God is to count as rationally justified. And because they feel challenged by them, they wonder whether they really are warranted in having their A/C-based beliefs, and cannot rest in these beliefs until that they have defeated the defeaters. Plantinga himself recognizes the need to defeat these potential defeaters, since, over and over again, he says that the theist's basic belief in God is internally rational only if they have done the best they can to think long and hard about all the issues surrounding their belief, which includes defeating these defeaters. Thus it turns out that for Quinn's scientifically sophisticated adults in our culture to have warrant for their basic belief in God they must have arguments against the potential defeaters. Does this requirement clash with Plantinga's repeated claim that a basic belief in God can be warranted even if the believer is unable to give any argument for his belief? Has Plantinga merely relocated the point at which the basic believer must appeal to arguments or evidential support, thereby creating the relocation problem?

Plantinga's response to this problem is that his basic believer need not give any argument or evidence for the existence of God and for his having set things up the way his A/C model says he has in order to defeat the potential defeaters. Plantinga has an easy time defeating the potential defeaters based on naturalistic explanations of religious belief. He convincingly argues that these challenges, such as those of Marx and Freud, can be defeated by showing that they presuppose the falsity of theism and moreover have little evidential support in their own right. The arguments from evil are the serious potential defeater to his A/C based beliefs. We saw in Chapter 3 that Plantinga has several strategies for countering these arguments, the major one of which was theistic skepticism, but this was found to be highly problematic. Another one of his strategies is to point out that the known evils of the world would not lower the probability that God exists if we had strong warrant for believing that God exists. If this warrant is based on theistic arguments, such as those found in Chapter 2, there is an appeal to evidence or argumentative support, and thus Plantinga has merely relocated the point at which such an appeal must be made. And if this warrant is supposed to come from A/C based beliefs, it can be objected that he has not shown that we have such warrant, only that it is possible that we have. And to show that we in fact have it, he would have to give arguments for the existence of God and his having instilled in us a *sensus divinitatis*, and thus an evidential appeal is made. It looks like Plantinga's *sensus divinitatis*-based beliefs cannot have basic warrant, since an appeal must be made to evidence or arguments in support of them.

PRAGMATIC JUSTIFICATIONS

There is another way of justifying a belief that has yet to be considered. It is the pragmatic way based on the desirable consequences that accrue to having the belief. The desirable consequences can be either prudential or moral. Blaise Pascal presented a famous "Wager Argument" to show that we are prudentially well advised to choose to believe that God exists, since we thereby advance our own self-interest. We cannot, in general, believe at will, voluntarily, on purpose, intentionally, and the like, but we can do things at will that will help to self-induce belief, such as having a hypnotist give us a post-hypnotic suggestion or someone brainwash us. The most commonly used causal recipe for self-inducing a belief is to act as if you believe. Pascal recommends that we acquire a belief in God by imitating the procedures that were followed by those who did succeed in acquiring this belief: Join the church, take the holy water, say the masses, and the like. To simplify our discussion, we will imagine that we have a surefire way of self-inducing a belief in any given proposition by popping a pill that will induce a belief in it.

Pascal likens deciding whether to believe that God exists to placing a wager. We bet on the basis of what the payoffs are on winning and losing and the probability of winning or losing. It would be unwise to confine ourselves to considerations of only payoffs, since then we would always bet on the horse that gives the highest yield on a winning ticket, which we know is a quick way to go broke at the track; however, if we could not make any use of probabilistic considerations, this would be the wise policy. And, according to Pascal, this is just the situation we are in with respect to God, the reason being that since we are finite and God is infinite we cannot have any epistemic justification for believing or disbelieving that God exists, nor can we even assign a higher probability to his existence than to his nonexistence. Since the odds are even, we should determine whether to believe that God exists (bet on the God horse) or that he does not exist (bet on the no-God horse) solely on the basis of the payoffs on winning and losing our belief-bet.

To determine these payoffs Pascal makes use of a religious creed that specifies how God rewards believers and/or punishes nonbelievers. According to this creed God treats agnostics and atheists alike with respect to payoffs, thereby eliminating the agnostic option of suspending belief. Thus our option is a forced one. It is a race on which you must wager. There are three versions of the Wager argument. The best case version makes use of an endless life in heaven but does not have nonbelievers placed in hell. The worst case version makes use of hell but not heaven, and the combined version avails itself of both heaven and hell. Given the horror that many present-day theists have at the thought of a merciful God assigning people to an endless life of suffering in hell, only the best case version will be considered.

According to this version if you win your belief-bet on God because he exists, the outcome has infinite value or utility; and, if you lose your bet, not only will you never find out that you have lost, your loss, if it is a loss at all, is only finite: You have wasted some time in church and been less rapacious in seeking your own worldly advantage. On the other hand, if you win your disbelief-bet, your payoff has only at best a finite value; and, if you lose your bet, given that there is no hell, the outcome has again only a finite value. Obviously, the smart money is on God, since you have the infinite to gain and only the finite to lose in a game where the odds of winning or losing are fifty-fifty, whereas if your no–God horse comes in, there is only at best a finite payoff.

It will not do to object that Pascal is enjoining us to act hypocritically by acting as if we believe when we really don't, for you would be acting hypocritically only if you pretended to believe. Nor is it to the point to object that Pascal's God would not reward someone with heaven who acquires a belief in him on prudential grounds; for, although it is true that the initial motivation for his acquiring belief is based on self-interest, it is his intention to wind up with a sincere, nonprudentially based belief. Given his present fallen condition, he must initially be motivated by self-interest, but by acquiring the belief he will change his character, what sort of motivations he has, so that they are no longer based on self-interest. Thus, the Pascalian wagerer is someone who wants to change his character.

What happens to Pascal's Wager if we do not grant him that it is just as likely as not that God exists. Maybe you were impressed by the arguments from evil and think that they significantly lower the probability, even to less than one-half, that God exists. The following rational choice theoretical version of his Wager can accommodate this possibility:

1. It is logically possible that God, as conceived of by Pascal's Christian creed, exists. Premise

2. The probability that this God exists is a finite number greater than zero. From 1

3. It is prudentially rational for a person to choose that option among those open to him that will maximize his expected gain. Premise

4. Believing that this God exists maximizes one's expected gain. Based on the Christian creed

5. It is prudentially rational for a person to choose to believe that this God exists. From 3 and 4

The expected gain of a given option is the sum of the expected utilities of its possible outcomes, with the expected utility of an outcome being the product of its probability and utility. Because Pascal eschewed probabilities, his Wager worked only with utilities. Given that there is an infinite utility if you win your belief-bet on God and the probability of winning is a finite number greater than zero, the expected utility of this outcome, along with the expected gain of the option to believe that God exists, is infinite. This is because the product of an infinite number and any finite number greater than zero is infinity. The expected gain for the option of not believing that God exists must be only finite, since the expected utility of winning on this option is finite.

There are powerful objections to this rational-choice version of the Wager, some of which also apply to the Wager sans probability. In the first place, from the fact that it is logically possible that God exists, it does not follow that the probability that he exists is a finite number greater than zero. In a fair lottery with a denumerable infinity of tickets, for each ticket it is logically possible that it will win, but the probability of its doing so is infinitesimal, and the product of an infinitesimal and an infinite number is infinitesimal. Thus, the expected gain of buying any ticket is infinitesimal. There is at least a denumerable infinity of logically possible deities who reward and/or punish believers in the manner described by the three versions of Pascal's Wager. For instance, there is the logically possible deity who rewards with infinite felicity all and only those who believe in him and step on only one sidewalk crack in the course of their life, as well as the two-crack deity, the three-crack deity, and so on ad infinitum.

It might be urged that it is still prudentially rational to believe in one of the rewarding and/or punishing deities, since, by doing so, one assures that it is logically possible that he realize the big utility and/or logically impossible that he realize the big disutility. The same response can be made on behalf of the Wager sans probability version when it is confronted with the infinitely-many-logically-possible-deities objection. The problem is that among the logically possible deities is the antitheistic deity who rewards with the big utility all and only those who believe in no rewarding and/or punishing deity and punishes all who do.

The only way of dealing with the problem posed by the infinitely-many-logically-possible-deities, as well as the possibility of the antitheistic God, is to resort to epistemological considerations that give favored status to some member of finite number of members of the former. This way out is not available to Pascal because of his negative theology, but there is no reason why the defender of the Wager argument must accept his negative theology. If we come out with a finite number of theistic Gods with equally good epistemic credentials, the prudential thing to do is to bet on any one of them or as many of them as you can consistently bet on or combine into a higher synthesis, thereby becoming the "religious hustler" who spends the weekend racing around town attending as many different religious services as possible, producing a higher synthesis when possible by, for example, not eating pork on Fridays. The expected gain on any of these finitely many theistic options is infinite, since now the probability of winning is no longer infinitesimal, while that of nonbelief is only finite. And, if it should turn out that the probability that one of these theistic Gods exists is greater than that for any of the others, it would be reasonable to supplement rational-choice theory with the ad hoc proviso that when two or more options have infinite expected utilities, the rational thing is to choose the one that has the highest probability of realizing the big utility (and/or avoiding the big disutility).

The epistemologically reinforced version of the Wager is not without difficulties. First, Pascal is being presumptuous in filling in our utility assignments for the different possible outcomes. As Swinburne correctly pointed out, Pascal assumed that all men would evaluate in the same way as he the various outcomes, but this is not in fact so. Pascal assumes that because the afterlife in a Christian heaven is one of infinite bliss or happiness without end all of us will assign it an infinite utility, but we can imagine Humphrey Bogart responding to this by saying, "Listen, Blaise, there are other things in life than infinite bliss, like doing right by a pal."

Many people would reject the value Pascal places on our worldly life vis-à-vis an eternal life of infinite bliss in a Christian heaven. He states that in opting to believe we risk losing only the finite—this worldly life—with the equal chance to gain an "infinity of life infinitely happy." He holds that "when there is the finite to hazard in a play where the chances of gain and loss are equal, and the infinite to gain" one has to be irrational not to play. But consider an existentialist who believes that the most important thing, that which has the highest utility assignment in his scheme of values, is that he lives this worldly life, which is the only one that he knows for sure he has, as authentically as possible. If he squanders this life by living in a manner that is not expressive of his true self, he risks losing everything. The loss, given his pecking order, is an infinite one in the sense of being the totality. It must be remembered in this connection that there is no neat correlation between the payoffs of the various outcomes and the utility that will be placed upon them by different persons. For instance, if a person has only two dollars and needs it to secure food so as to survive, he might well refuse to gamble this sum even if he has an equal chance to win an infinite or as-large-as-you-please number of dollars. This person would not give the highest or infinite utility assignment to the winning outcome.

The question, then, is whether the worldly life of those who accept the Wager is an authentic one for them. For some it is and for others not. There are those free spirits who think that they would not be true to themselves if they were to adopt the authoritarian orientation that is required of an active, believing member of most of the world's leading religions. The restrictions that this would entail in regard to how they must think, feel, and act would be anathema to them.

On the other hand, there are those for whom the religious way of life is authentic and self-fulfilling. They are the sort who would want to pursue this religious way of life even if it did not lead on to the big afterlife payoff. They agree with Pascal that you will gain by it in this life. In the great extant religions of the world, which are the only live or practically possible religious options for the vast majority of people, worldly means and afterlife ends are of a piece, forming an integral unity. In Christianity, for example, heavenly existence is just a more intense and refined version of the worldly religious life in which one's relation to God, since not encumbered by the body, is an unceasing beatific or mystic vision of his true positive nature. Only people who find the Christian way of life attractive would find an unending survival in a Christian heaven especially valuable. Their reason, accordingly, for believing that God exists is not a pragmatic one based on its being a means to some desirable end, but that they want to be people of faith, the religious way of life having an intrinsic value for them.

Thus, Pascal's Wager is not really a wager, since the people who accept it do not see themselves as *gambling* at all. According to their scheme of preferences, they are not *risking* something finite, their worldly life, for the chance of gaining some infinite otherworldly reward, since the religious way of life is the one that has the greatest value for them. Pascal's Wager turns out to be nothing but a pep talk to those who suffer from weakness of will. They find the religious way of life attractive (and thereby the afterlife to which it supposedly leads) but cannot get themselves to make the requisite commitment because of counteracting traits of their present character. They are in the same situation as those who want to change their character but find it difficult because they must overcome the counterbalancing force of formed habits. They need a pep talk so that they can strengthen and make dominant their second-order intention to change their first-order motivations and reasons for acting.

This concludes our discussion of the prudential version of the consequentialist justification of theistic belief and we will now turn to its moral version as formulated by William James in his famous and highly disputed essay of 1896, "The Will to Believe," which is based on the morally desirable consequences of a theistic belief. I will present a refined and strengthened version of his will-to-believe doctrine. The very idea of believing because of the good consequences of doing so causes many philosophers to take off the safety switch on their shotguns, among whom is C. K. Clifford who laid down this universal moral prohibition against believing on any basis other than an evidential one: "It is wrong always, everywhere, and for anyone, to believe anything upon insufficient evidence." This allegedly scientific credo served as the polemical target of James's essay. He not only wanted to produce counterexamples to it, the most exciting of which is an evidentially nonwarranted belief in God, but also spell out the general conditions under which one is morally permitted to believe upon insufficient evidence. Before we present these conditions, we should look at the arguments that have been advanced in support of this credo.

Clifford's defense of the credo is based on an act utilitarian moral theory and attempts to show that the full, long-term consequences of *any* evidentially nonwarranted belief are disastrous. Such a belief might maximize utility in the short-run by making you feel good, such as my present belief that I am the sultan of Wisconsin (No one cuts the cheese in Wisconsin without my approval!), but in the long-run it won't. The reason is that in allowing yourself to acquire or retain this one belief you take the first step that inevitably will result in your acquiring the habit of believing in this way. This is most unfortunate, since, in general, evidentially nonwarranted beliefs prevent one from getting around successfully in the world: We would not survive, no less survive well, unless our beliefs generally were true. The example that you set in being credulous and gullible will then spread like a plague to the rest of your community. This will result in humanity sinking back into barbarism and savagery, to use Clifford's bloated rhetoric.

It should be obvious that Clifford's plague theory wildly exaggerates the deleterious consequences of having an evidentially nonwarranted belief. There are, however, less dubious ways of supporting his credo. One begins with the fact that false belief is an evil, an ought-not-to-be. The best way to prevent this evil is to not believe upon insufficient evidence, which is just what Clifford's credo requires. But, you might ask, why is false belief an evil? One answer appeals to the Aristotelian doctrine of natural law, which holds that the good for each individual is to actualize its essence. The essence of man is rationality, being that which sets him apart from the rest of the animal kingdom and gives him a special value and dignity. To be rational requires having true beliefs, and this is best realized by obeying the Clifford credo.

There is enough force to the utilitarian and natural law defenses of the credo so as to place the onus on one who violates it to justify doing so. In other words, we have a prima facie duty not to believe upon insufficient evidence, but, being prima facie, this duty is defeasible, meaning that anyone who violates this duty must be able to produce a good reason, a defeating condition, for doing so. One sort of defeater involves believing in the trustworthiness of the person with whom you have a trust relationship. A husband, for example, ought to believe in the faithfulness of his wife even if he has not gathered sufficient evidence for this belief. In fact, the very attempt to gather such evidence, say by hiring a private detective to trail her, violates the trust relationship.

Another type of defeater involves a case in which one can bring about (or prevent) some great good (or evil) by having an evidentially nonwarranted belief. Imagine that the ETs come to earth and tell us that they will eliminate all disease, poverty, and war if Jones acquires the evidentially nonwarranted belief that Cleopatra weighed 104 pounds when she died. Or they might threaten to obliterate us if he doesn't. Let's hope that Jones pops the belief-inducing pill!

Clifford's credo can accommodate these two recalcitrant cases if it is downgraded from an absolute to this prima facie moral obligation: It is *prima facie* wrong always, everywhere, and for anyone, to believe anything upon insufficient evidence. These two cases would be recognized as defeaters of this prima facie duty. But could a case of believing that God exists upon insufficient evidence also qualify as an exception to the credo? James attempts to show that under special conditions it can. What he does is, first, spell out the general conditions for being a defeater or exception to our prima facie duty to obey the credo and, then, go on to show that an evidentially nonwarranted belief in God could satisfy all of these conditions.

These are the amended and strengthened Jamesian sufficient conditions for a person, A, being morally permitted at time, T, to believe an epistemically nonwarranted proposition, p:

1. To believe p and to not believe p are each real possibilities for A at T;

2. Whether or not A believes p will vitally affect A's future life;

3. The circumstances are such that if A does not decide to believe p, A will not believe p;

4. It is practically impossible at T for A to decide on epistemological grounds the truth of p;

5. A's believing p can help A to bring it about that q becomes true, in which q is not identical with p;

6. It is morally desirable that q become true;

7. A's psychology at T is such that A can realize the confidence and courage boosting benefits of a belief that p, even if he takes p to be evidentially nonwarranted;

8. A knows that he will act so as to help make q become true if and only if he believes in advance that p is true;

9. A's belief that p is a rational reason for him to act so as to help make q become true.

It is necessary that each of these conditions be explained. Then we can see how they apply to an evidentially nonwarranted belief in God.

1. This condition requires that A has an open mind at T with respect to p, considering it to be both a real possibility that it is true and a real possibility that it is false. For those who, to use James's delightful phrase, are not among the saving remnant because they are dyed-in–the-wool atheists, the proposition that God exists is not a live belief-option. The liveliness of a proposition can vary from one person to another and from one time in a person's life to another. The dyed-in-the-wool atheist might have been willing to entertain at some earlier time in his life the real possibility that God exists.

2. Whether or not A believes p will have momentous consequences for him, because his psychology at T is such that what he believes in this matter will vitally affect how he behaves in the future. As with condition 1, this varies across persons and across times in a single person's life. It is momentous for a person whether or not he believe that God exists, if what he believes about this will determine his general orientation to the world. But for someone with a different psychology, someone who will live in pretty much the same way whatever he believes about God's existence, this would not be a momentous belief-option.

3. What this condition says is that A's belief-option is a forced one in that if he makes no choice at all, he will wind up with the negative alternative, not believing that p. No one, such as a crazed brain surgeon or mad cyberneticist, is going to compel him to have this belief regardless of what he might do. It is completely up to A whether or not he acquires the belief that p. Recall that for Pascal the option to bet on God is a forced option, since if you do not place any bet, you wind up with the same outcome as if you had bet on the no-God horse. Dated options, such as to accept a proposal of marriage by midnight tomorrow or never see the man again, are good examples of forced options. A forced option need not be momentous, which would be the case if this proposal were offered to a lesbian.

4. This condition is necessary for meeting the all too common objection to James's will-to-believe doctrine that it licenses wishful thinking. It is not enough that the evidence available to A at T is adequate neither for the truth of p nor for the falsity of p. A must be in this position of epistemic undecidability after he has done his best to determine the truth of p. We know of far too many cases of self-serving ignorance in the corporate world, such as ValueJet's claim that they did not have any evidence that their plane that crashed was defective. I am not morally permitted to believe that I am the sultan of Wisconsin, even if it satisfies conditions 1–3, for I could find out that this is false.

There are stronger and weaker versions of the epistemic unde-cidability requirement. The strongest version requires a tie, that the evidence available to A at T, *after an adequate inquiry has been performed*, favors neither p nor not-p. A weaker version requires only that the evidence for p or for not-p is not overwhelming. Maybe the strength of the epistemic undecidability requirement should vary inversely with the momentousness of the belief-option. For the Jamesian "sick souls" who have a desperate need to believe in God, this requirement might be set very low. But the weaker the requirement, the less convincing is the case as a counterinstance to the Clifford credo. Fortunately, as will be shown, James can make do with the strong requirement.

5. Imagine that you are stranded in the Alps and can get to safety only by jumping across a ravine. You have no evidence about your chances of succeeding, since you have never attempted this long a jump before. Let p be the conditional proposition that if you attempt the jump, you will succeed, and q be the proposition that you will successfully make the jump. Most people's psychology is such that by believing p they help to bring it about that q will become true. We can think of numerous such confidence- and courage-building beliefs. Most people are so psychologically constituted that by believing that they have the capacity to succeed in some endeavor, such as succeeding in law school, winning the heart of some lady, winning a tennis match, they help to bring it about that they do. James believed that we could psych ourselves up to lead the morally strenuous life if we first believed this conditional proposition:

> R. If we collectively exert our best moral effort, then good
> will win out over evil in the long run.

A belief in R will give many people the courage and confidence to promote good and fight evil, thereby helping to cause it to be the case that

> q. Good will win out over evil in the long run.

Our best collective moral efforts are not alone a sufficient cause of q's becoming true, but they are at least a contributory cause. We need as well the assistance of the friendly forces within nature, which James called "God." In promoting this conception of a finite God James went so far as to say that the proposition that God exist is identical with R.

It is important to stress that in these courage- and confidence-building cases what is required is honest to God, all out, sweating with conviction belief. Merely adopting p as a working hypothesis or hoping it is true will not suffice. Our Alpine jumper won't be aided in making a successful jump if he merely adopts as a working hypothesis that he has the ability to do so or hopes he can. But imagine that he can get to safety only by following just one of three paths that are available to him but does not have any evidence that favors one of them over the others. The rational thing to do is to form the working hypothesis with respect to one of them that it will lead to safety and then follow it: Your success does not depend upon your believing that it is the right path. All that matters is that you move one foot after the other. In science we often adopt an evidentially nonwarranted proposition as a working hypothesis for the purpose of programming experiments without having to believe it is true; however, there are cases in the history of science in which it proved valuable that a scientist passionately believed in his pet working hypothesis which subsequently got verified, because it enabled him to persevere when others would have given up. It is interesting to note that whereas Christianity requires honest to God, all-out, sweating with conviction belief in the proposition that God exists, orthodox Judaism requires only that it be adopted as a working hypothesis for the purpose of following various prescribed laws and rules.

6. James is attempting to concoct a case that is a moral defeater for Clifford's credo. Therefore, it is required that the proposition q that A is attempting to help make true by acquiring a belief in the conditional proposition, p (that if he does some action, this will help to make q become true), report something that is morally desirable. It is morally desirable that A will successfully jump across the ravine, that good will win out over evil in the long run, and so on. James's will-to-believe justification is a substitution instance of this argument form:

Doing x helps to bring it about that p.

It is morally desirable that p. Therefore,

It is prima facie morally permissible to do x.

in which "believing that p" is substituted for "x" throughout. The reason for the prima facie qualification is that the moral permission is subject to potential defeaters or overriders. For example, that p becomes true might promote something that is morally good yet bring about in its wake an outweighing evil. Or its becoming true might violate some overriding moral duty, as in the case in which I promise to give Jones a revolver but in the interim he turns into a homicidal maniac and will kill some innocent person if I do so. My giving Jones a revolver helps to bring it about that I keep my promise, and that I keep my promise is morally desirable. But my prima facie moral permission to give Jones a revolver is defeated, because doing so would result in the death of an innocent person.

7. This condition is needed to meet certain objections. Dickenson Miller claimed that it is impossible to believe a proposition that you take to be evidentially nonwarranted, for then you would be uncertain and thus not believe. But, *pace* this objection, one can believe a proposition is true without taking it to be certain. Think of the many anti-rationalistic theists of the Kierkegaardian variety who believe that God exists but think that there their belief is irrational on epistemic grounds. Richard Swinburne, therefore, was wrong to claim that to believe a proposition is to believe that its probability is greater than one-half relative to the available evidence. I can believe that a certain horse will win even though I know that the probability that it will is less than one-half.

A more interesting objection is that if one believes what he takes to be evidentially unfounded, he will not, *pace* James, have his confidence and courage boosted by this belief, and thus A's belief that p is true will not aid him in his endeavor to help make q become true. The wrong response to this objection is to find some procedure for making the believer forget that he acquired his belief on the basis of a will-to-believe option, say, by ingesting a pill that will make him forget the nonrational means by which he acquired this belief and instead implant in his mind the false apparent memory of having acquired it after a successful empirical inquiry. The problem with this way around the objection is that the believer must deceive himself, which is bad enough, but in the process destroys his own integral unity and winds up as a divided, schizophrenic self. The ideal of an integrated, rational self is a powerful one that deserves more respect than is accorded it by this drastic solution.

A better response is that human psychology is far more variable than this objection envisions. Although it is true that there are some people who are so constituted psychologically that they cannot realize the confidence-building benefits from a belief that they take to be evidentially nonwarranted, there are many people whose psychology permits them to do so, such as our nonrationalist theists. It has already been seen that a will-to-believe option is relative to a person at a time because human psychology is variable in regard to which propositions a person takes to be live and momentous belief options. All this objection shows is that there is another psychological reason for relativizing a will-to-believe option to a person at a time. Thus, we must add condition 7 requiring that A's psychology at T is such that he can realize the confidence and courage boosting benefits of a belief that p, even if he takes p to be evidentially nonwarranted.

8. This condition results from the need to meet the objection that A could do his best to make q become true without believing in advance that p is true. For example, he could do his best to bring it about that good will win out over evil in the long run by performing altruistic actions even though he doesn't believe in advance that if we collectively exert our best moral effort, then good will win out over evil in the long run. Some people need confidence boosters, others do not. There is an easy way around this objection that consists in building in yet another epicycle concerning the way in which a will–to–believe option must be relativized to a person's psychological makeup at the time of the choice, namely, A knows at T that he will act so as to help make q become true only if he first believe that p is true. The reason why A must know this psychological fact about himself is that the conditions for having a will–to–believe option are supposed to justify A's believing or acquiring the belief that p. But what justifies a belief gives the believer a reason for so believing, something that he could give in response to the challenge to justify his belief. This requires that he be aware of this reason or justification.

9. Among A's reasons for acting so as to make q become true is his belief that p is true. It is necessary that this belief is a rational reason for his so acting; for, if it were not, he would not be acting in a free, rational manner and thus would not qualify as a morally responsible agent. This is a very serious matter, given the great importance we place upon being such an agent, that could well serve as a defeater to his being morally permitted to believe p upon insufficient evidence. Imagine that A has a very screwed up psychology. He will act so as to help good win out over evil in the long urn only if he first believes that Verdi composed *Ernani*. Because of the irrationality of this reason, he would not be performing his good–making actions as a free, rational, morally responsible agent, thus the need for the additional condition that requires that A's belief that p is a rational reason for him to act so as to help make q become true.

Having completed the task of explaining each of the conditions in James's set of sufficient conditions for being morally permitted to believe upon insufficient evidence, it can be determined whether a belief that God exists could satisfy them. It is not hard to cook the circumstances so that A's belief that God exists satisfies 1–9. The option to believe that God exists could be live and momentous, as well as forced, for A, as it is for many people. That condition 4 can be satisfied is more controversial, since it requires us to grant that neither theism nor atheism is epistemically justified. In the light of the inconclusiveness of our lengthy discussion in Chapters 2 and 3 of the attempts to epistemically justify theism and atheism, this is not an unreasonable claim. James, for one, believed this.

A's belief that God exists, obviously, cannot help to make it true that God exists, so what morally desirable proposition, q, can it help to make true? It could be that A acts in an altruistic, good–making fashion, since A's psychology at T could be such that he will act in this way, and knows that he will, only if he first believes that God exists. His reason for so acting could be prudential, if it were motivated by his belief that God will reward him for doing so. Although a prudential reason is not the best reason for so acting, it still is a rational reason, for it is rational to act so as to promote one's own self-interest. Or he might have the nonprudential reason that so acting will make him more God-like. There are many other forms that q can take. It might be that he will become healthier and happier. Or it could even be that some evidence for the existence will be unearthed. The reason is that by believing that God exists, A increases his chance of having an M-experience—an apparent direct nonsensory perception of God—and this would constitute some evidence for the existence of God. As we know from the discussion in Chapter 2 of Alston's analogical argument for the cognitivity of M-experiences, this is highly controversial. There is no problem in imagining that A's psychology at time T satisfies conditions 7 and 8.

In accordance with the tennis match approach of this book, some objections will be raised to James's will-to-believe doctrine. The first objection is that this doctrine violates the principle of the universality of moral propositions—that if it is morally obligatory (forbidden, permitted) for person A to do X, then it is morally obligatory (forbidden, permitted) for anyone to do X. The reason is that A could satisfy conditions 1–9 and thereby be morally permitted to believe p upon insufficient evidence, but another person, B, whose psychology differs from A's in that B does not need to believe p in order to act so as to help make q become true, does not have this moral permission. Because A satisfies condition 8 and B does not, A has a moral permission that B lacks, which violates the principle of the universality of moral propositions.

Phil Quinn attempted to rebut this objection by correctly pointing out that the universalization of a moral claim requires that the people who are covered by the generalization are in relevantly similar circumstances. The proper formulation of the universalization principle is: If it is morally obligatory (forbidden, permitted) for person A to do X in circumstance C, then it is morally obligatory (forbidden, permitted) for anyone to do X in circumstance C. Thus, as Quinn rightfully claims, it is possible that I have a moral permission to kill a human being because this is the only way I can prevent my being murdered by a maniac, but you would not be justified in killing someone because you are not in such dire circumstances.

The only remaining question is whether condition 8— *A* knows that he will act so as to help make *q* true if and only if he believes in advance that *p* is true—specifies a morally relevant circumstance so that a person who fails to satisfy it would fail to have the same moral permission to believe upon insufficient evidence that is had by a person who satisfies it. But it seems wrong to accord a moral privilege to someone but not another on the grounds that their psychologies differ. Consider a confidence building case. *A* is a psychologically weaker person than *B* in that *A*, but not *B*, needs the confidence-building belief that *p* is true before he can get himself to act effectively so as to help to make *q* become true. Why should the fact that *A* is weaker than *B* give him a moral permission that *B* lacks?

Quinn responds that the difference between *A*'s and *B*'s psychology is morally relevant, the reason being that this difference by itself explains why one person has a moral permission that the other does not. This response is a good example of one person's *modus ponens* being the basis for another person's *modus tollens*. Quinn constructs this *modus ponens* argument:

1. If a condition is such that a person who satisfies it has a moral permission that someone who does not satisfy it lacks, then this condition is a morally relevant circumstance;
2. Condition 8 is such that a person who satisfies it has a moral permission that someone who does not satisfy it lacks; therefore,
3. Condition 8 is a morally relevant circumstance.

This argument really constitutes a *reductio ad absurdum* of premise 2. The obvious falsity of 3, the argument's conclusion, sets the stage for this *modus tollens* argument for the negation of premise 2:

1. If a condition is such that a person who satisfies it has a moral permission that someone who does not satisfy it lacks, then this condition is a morally relevant circumstance;
2. Condition 8 is not a morally relevant circumstance; therefore,

3. It is false that condition 8 is such that a person who
satisfies it has a moral permission that someone who
does not satisfy it lacks.

Quinn's *modus ponens* argument is not sufficiently discriminating
since it can be used to prove too much. For example, suppose
we add another necessary condition to 1–9—that one must have
red hair. Quinn's argument could then be used to show that this is
a morally relevant circumstance, for it alone would explain why
someone with red hair has a moral permission to believe upon
insufficient evidence that a person without red hair lacks. Again,
we have a *modus ponens* argument that should be converted to a
modus tollens argument. In order to determine whether it should be
a *modus ponens* or *modus tollens* argument we must appeal to our
pre-analytic intuitions about what is a morally relevant circumstance. We recognize that being in a kill or be killed circumstance
is a morally relevant circumstance but that being red haired or
unconfident or weak willed is not.

There is a much more effective way of rebutting the universalizability objection that Quinn pursues. He reminds us that conditions
1–9 are only *sufficient* for being morally permitted to believe upon
insufficient evidence. Because they are not claimed to be *necessary* as
well, a person who does not satisfy one of the included conditions is
not thereby denied this moral permission. Thus, B, is not *denied* the
moral permission to believe p upon insufficient in virtue of his not
satisfying condition 7. He only is not given it.

This way around the universalizability objection is too facile.
In the first place, it seems to commit the sin of making what
condition 8 specifies a morally relevant circumstance, since A, in
virtue of satisfying it, has a moral permission that B, in virtue of
not satisfying it, does not have, even though he is not *denied* this
permission. The response to this might be that you are morally
permitted to do whatever you are not morally prohibited from
doing. Since B is not morally prohibited from believing p upon
insufficient evidence, since conditions 1–9 are only sufficient, he is
morally permitted to do so. But you are not morally permitted to
do X when you are *prima facie* morally prohibited from doing X.
And since Clifford's credo seemed to be acceptable when it was
downgraded to a prima facie moral prohibition against having an
evidentially nonwarranted belief, B is prima facie morally prohibited from believing p upon insufficient evidence.

If the universalizability principle is to be saved, we must find some defeating circumstance that frees B from being bound by his prima facie duty to obey Clifford's credo. B, *ex hypothesis*, is not in a trust relationship or an extreme utilitarian situation, so these defeaters are not available to him as a justification for his believing p upon insufficient evidence. What could this additional defeating condition be? I leave it to the reader to find this defeater, since I'm not up to doing so. I hope it can be found. If it can't be found, the universalizability objection has not been laid to rest.

So far we have considered attempts to pragmatically justify theistic belief in terms of its desirable consequences, be they prudential or moral. But there have been numerous attempts to pragmatically discredit theistic belief and to show that atheistic belief has better overall consequences than theistic belief. The history of theistic belief is a mixed bag, containing what is both highest and lowest in human behavior. We are familiar with these good consequences—sainthood, compassion, charity, love, devotion, courage, and the like. But we are also familiar with its basest consequences, especially in its exclusivist form—persecutions, holy wars, prejudice, bigotry, arrogance, smugness, and the like: Even the Holocaust can be partially attributed to exclusivist Christian belief. An exclusivist religious belief is one that entails that *all* religious creeds other than the one of which it is a creedal part are mistaken in some of their fundamental creedal beliefs. An example of such a belief is that God is triune and that only those who believe this will find salvation. An attempt will now be made to mount a pragmatic argument against exclusivist religious beliefs that get publicized and promulgated that is based on a modified version of James's will-to-believe doctrine.

James's will-to-believe doctrine attempted to show how one could be morally *permitted* to believe (or continue to believe) without sufficient epistemic warrant; however, it quite plausibly can be extended so as to show under what conditions one is morally *forbidden* to believe without sufficient epistemic warrant, namely cases in which believing without sufficient epistemic warrant will have morally undesirable consequences. After this extended version of James's will-to-believe doctrine is developed, it will be deployed against exclusivist theistic beliefs that get publicized and promulgated. The reason for this restriction will become manifest.

The following is an extended will-to-believe type argument for one being morally forbidden to have (or continue to have) an exclusivist theistic belief.

1. For any proposition, *p*, if one cannot show that *p* is epistemically warranted and the consequences of believing *p* are worse than they would have been if one were not to have believed *p*, then one morally ought not to believe *p*. Premise

2. An exclusivist theistic proposition cannot be shown to be epistemically warranted. Premise

3. The consequences of believing an exclusivist theistic proposition are worse than they would have been if one were not to have believed it. Premise

4. One morally ought not to believe an exclusivist religious proposition. From 1, 2, and 3 by modus ponens and universal instantiation

This hardly is a decisive argument. Its premises call for further clarification and support.

The use of "epistemically warranted" in premise 1 and 2, for the sake of argument, will recognize two species of epistemic warrant. One is the familiar notion of Lockean *evidential warrant* from Chapters 2 and 3 and the other Plantinga's previously discussed notion of *basic warrant* according to which a belief is basically warranted if it is not based on or inferred from another belief and results from the proper functioning of one's cognitive faculties in the right kind of epistemic environment according to a design plan successfully aimed at truth.

If premise 1 did not contain the caveat, "if one cannot show that *p* is epistemically warranted," it would not be acceptable to those who believe that our essence as rational beings requires us to base our beliefs on the best available evidence, at least when it can be had. The good of our believing in a way that is epistemically justified trumps whatever evil might result from this. This valid point will upset those who are obsessed with political correctness and multiculturalism and think that we should not publicly express any belief, however well epistemically founded, that will in any way harm someone. One doesn't have to be an Aristotelian natural law theorist to disagree, since the utilitarian consequences of adopting their policy would be disastrous. But premise 1, with the caveat "if one cannot show that p is epistemically warranted," seems self-evident, being a special instance of our duty not to bring about what is evil. For an evil is an ought-not-to-be and thus we ought not to bring about what we ought not to bring about. This is a tautology but at least it's true. Some might oppose premise 1 by appealing to our having a moral duty to believe the truth, whatever the consequences might be. We have this duty but it doesn't challenge 1; for 1 is concerned with the basis on which we ought to go about forming our beliefs, and this duty gives us no practical guidance in this endeavor.

Premise 2 is highly controversial, since there are those, such as Richard Swinburne, who argue that exclusivist Christian beliefs are evidentially warranted. To do this it must be shown that the Bible is a divine revelation, and this is too big an issue to go into here. Even if the theistic arguments in Chapter 2 succeeded in showing that theistic belief is epistemically justified, it would be a long way from showing that some particular exclusivist theistic belief is. Alvin Plantinga, as we saw earlier in this chapter, argued only that it is *possible* that we that we have basic warrant for believing an exclusivist theistic proposition, not that we actually have. To prove the latter requires showing that God exists and has instilled in us a *sensus divinitatis* as part of our original cognitive equipment and directly causes exclusivist theistic beliefs in us about the great things of the Gospel through the internal instigation of the Holy Spirit.

Premise 3 does not admit of any straightforward verification. In the first place, it is very difficult, if not impossible, to total up the goods and evils that have actually resulted from exclusivist religious beliefs; however, given that most of the evils in the present world result from religious exclusivism, it intuitively seems that the evils of such beliefs outweigh the goods. I say "intuitively" because we are unable to quantify good and evil. But even if the evils "outweigh" the goods, this does not settle the issue in favor of 3; for we might have a Hobson's Choice with respect to having an exclusivist religious belief, the consequences of each alternative being over-all bad, in which case we should select the alternative that has the least bad consequences. Thus, we must consider what would have happened in the counterfactual situation in which there are no exclusivist religious beliefs. Would things have gone better or worse than they did in the past history of the actual world? Again, a strain is put on our verificatory capacities.

James, for one, would not be phased by these verificatory complications, since he makes it quite clear in *The Varieties of Religious Experience* (VRE) that he fully and passionately accepts premise 3. In fact, James's basic intention in writing the *Varieties*, which was to show that the essence of religion consists in personal religious experiences rather than in religious institutions and their creeds, is driven by his abhorrence of what results from institutionalized exclusivist religions, as is amply borne out by the following quotations:

> Certainly the unhesitating and unreasoning way in which we feel that we must inflict our Civilization upon "lower" races, by means of Hotchkiss guns, etc., reminds one of nothing so much as of the early spirit of Islam spreading its religion by the sword (VRE 69).

> A survey of history shows us that, as a rule, religious geniuses attract disciples, and produce groups of sympathizers. When these groups get strong enough to "organize" themselves, they become ecclesiastical institutions with corporate ambitions of their own. The spirit of politics and the lust of dogmatic rule are then apt to enter and to contaminate the originally innocent thing; so that when we hear the word "religion" nowadays, we think inevitably of some "church" or other; and to some persons the word "church" suggests so much hypocrisy and tyranny and meanness and tenacity of superstition that in a wholesale undiscerning way they glory in saying that they are "down" on religion altogether (VRE 268–9).

James locates the cause of this institutional exclusivizing and dogmatizing what were originally vital personal religious experiences in our "spirit of corporate dominion." And when this is combined with our "spirit of dogmatic dominion" it leads to horrible evils.

It should now be clear why my will-to-believe argument against exclusivist theistic beliefs was restricted to those that get publicly promulgated, for it is through their publicity that repressive, exclusivist religions get founded, with all the horrendous evils that result from this, as witnessed in the world today. What we desperately need to do is to find some vital common denominator between the world's great extant religions so that their creeds can be revised in an ecumenical manner. These religions can retain in their creed features that are due to their unique history and culture, since God can truly reveal himself under different guises to differently circumstanced people at different times and places. This does not mean that any religion goes, as an extreme language-game fideist would maintain. For, as argued earlier in this chapter, there are moral and empirical grounds for challenging a religion. A religious ecumenicalist is well within his rights in rejecting religions that don't pass muster in these respects. If we don't find some way to ecumenicalize our religions, the future of humanity, if there is to be one at all, is a bleak one.

Suggested Readings

chapter 1

An in-depth treatment of atheological arguments is found in Richard M. Gale's *On the Nature and Existence of God* (New York; Cambridge Univ. Press, 1991). Antony Flew's *God and Philosophy* (Amherst: Prometheus Books, 2005) argues for the incoherence of theism. A very able response is contained in Richard Swinburne's *The Coherence of Theism* (Oxford: Oxford Univ. Press, 1977). For an account of process theology's concept of a finite God see Charles Hartshorne's *The Divine Reality* (New Haven: Yale Univ. Press, 1948). Nelson Pike's *God and Time* (Ithaca: Cornell Univ. Press, 1970) is a seminal discussion of the dispute between the friends and foes of God's timeless eternality. Defenses of God's timeless eternality are given by: Eleonore Stump and Norman Kretzman, "Eternity," *Journal of Philosophy* 78 (1981) 429–58; Paul Helm, *Eternal God* (New York: Oxford Univ. Press, 1988); and Brian Leftow, *Time and Eternity* (Ithaca: Cornell Univ. Press, 1991). A heated debate over the nature of God's eternality is in *God and Time*, edited by Gregory Ganssle (Downers Grove: Intervarsity Press, 2001), with Paul Helm defending God's timeless eternality against the assaults of the omnitemporalists, William Lane Craig, Alan Padgett, and Nicholas Wolterstorff.

chapter 2

Graham Oppy's *Ontological Arguments and Belief in God* (Cambridge: Cambridge Univ. Press, 1995) is a remarkable critical examination of virtually everything that has been published in English on this argument. Insightful discussions of this argument are: David Lewis, "Anselm and Actuality," *Nous* 4 (1970) 175–88; and Peter van Inwagen, "Indexicality and Actuality," *Philosophical Review* 89 (1980) 403–26. The most readable formulation of the modal ontological argument is in Alvin Plantinga's *God, Freedom, and Evil* (New York: Harper Torchbooks, 1974). Important treatments of the cosmological argument are: William Rowe, *The Cosmological Argument* (Princeton: Princeton Univ. Press, 1975); and William Lane Craig, *The Kalam Cosmological Argument* (London: Macmillan, 1979). A strengthened cosmological argument is given by Richard M. Gale and Alexander Pruss in "A New Cosmological Argument," *Religious Studies* 35 (1999) 461–76. Criticisms of this argument are found in essays by Graham Oppy and by Kevin Davey and Robert Clifton in 2001, with a response from Gale and Pruss in 2002, of *Religious Studies*. For a Bayesian attempt to agglomerate all of the teleological arguments so as to tip the balance in favor of the probability of God's existence see Richard Swinburne, *The Existence of God* (Oxford: Oxford Univ. Press, 1979). Elliot Sober's "The Design Argument," in *The Blackwell Guide to the Philosophy of Religion*, edited by William Mann (Oxford: Blackwell, 2005) is an excellent critical discussion of design arguments based on probability theory. A powerful attack on theistic arguments is given by Michael Martin in his *Atheism* (Philadelphia: Temple Univ. Press, 1990). Two excellent defenses of the cognitivity of mystical experiences are: William Alston, *Perceiving God* (Ithaca: Cornell Univ. Press, 1991); and William Wainwright, *Mysticism* (Madison: Univ. of Wisconsin Press, 1981). Their positions are criticized by Richard M. Gale in "On the Cognitivity of Mystical Experiences," *Faith and Philosophy* 22 (2005).

chapter 3

For a free will defense employing middle knowledge and for one that does not see, respectively: Plantinga, *God, Freedom, and Evil, op. cit.*; and Robert M. Adams, "Middle Knowledge and the Problem of Evil," *American Philosophical Quarterly* 14 (1977) 109–17. Their defenses are criticized by Richard M. Gale in "Freedom and the Free Will Defense," *Social Theory and Practice* 16 (1990), 397–423. A good seminal discussion of the evidential problem of evil is Bruce Russell and Stephen Wykstra, "The Inductive Argument from Evil: A Dialogue," *Philosophical Topics* 16 (1988) 133–60. *The Evidential Argument from Evil*, edited by Daniel Howard-Snyder (Bloomington: Indiana University Press, 1996) contains important essays by Rowe, Alston, Swinburne, Plantinga, van Inwagen, Stump, Russell, Wykstra, and Paul Draper. John Hick's soul-building theodicy is given in his *Evil and the God of Love* (New York: Harper and Row, 1966).

chapter 4

Antony Kenny defends nonliteralism in *The Unknown God* (London: Continuum, 2004). Language-game fideism is defended in: Ludwig Wittgenstein, *Lectures and Conversations*, edited by Cyril Barrett (Berkeley: Univ. of California Press); D. Z. Phillips, "Philosophy, Theology and the Reality of God," *The Philosophical Quarterly* 13 (1963), 344–50; and Norman Malcolm, "The Groundlessness of Belief," in *Reason and Religion*, edited by Stuart Brown (Ithaca: Cornell Univ. Press, 1977). A sharp attack on language-game fideism is given in Kai Nielsen's *An Introduction to the Philosophy of Religion* (New York: St. Martin's Press, 1982). Almost every set of readings in the philosophy of religion, among which are anthologies edited by Baruch Brody, Louis Pojman, and Rowe and Wainwright, contain C. K. Clifford, "The Ethics of Belief" and William James, "The Will to Believe." A valuable essay on religious pluralism and exclusivism is William Wainwright's "Competing Religious Claims" in *The Blackwell Guide to the Philosophy of Religion, op. cit.*